A CLEAR
PREMONITION

A CLEAR PREMONITION

The Letters of Lt Tim Lloyd
to his mother

Italy and North Africa 1943–4

Edited and with commentary
by
Raleigh Trevelyan
in collaboration with
Sampson Lloyd

LEO COOPER
LONDON

First published in Great Britain in 1995 by
LEO COOPER
190 Shaftesbury Avenue, London WC2H 8JL
an imprint of
Pen & Sword Books Ltd,
47 Church Street, Barnsley, South Yorkshire S70 2AS

A CIP catalogue record for this book is available
from the British Library

ISBN 0 85052 424 5

Typeset by Phoenix Typesetting,
Ilkley, West Yorkshire
in 11/13pt Linotype Sabon
Printed by
Redwood Books Ltd,
Trowbridge, Wilts

CONTENTS

ACKNOWLEDGEMENTS

Our thanks are due to the following for help in various ways: Mr and Mrs David Lloyd, Mrs Peter Lewis, Mrs Jack Flower, Baroness Ryder of Warsaw, Major Ron Cassidy, Alan Clipston, Tony Cressweller, Michael King, Michael Trevor-Williams, Janet Venn-Brown, Lady Whitaker, Alan Wyndham-Green.

Passages from *Child of My Love* by Sue Ryder (Collins Harvill, 1986) and *Beyond the Pale* by Nicholas Mosley (Martin Secker and Warburg, 1983) are quoted with the kind permission of the authors.

The illustrations are the copyright of Sampson Lloyd apart from the following: 14 and 16 with the kind permission of Sue Ryder: 8, 9, 10 and 15 Raleigh Trevelyan; 18 and 19 the Imperial War Museum; 24 and 25 from *With the Allied Armies in Italy* by Edward Seago, Collins 1945, the Seago Estate with grateful thanks.

EDITOR'S NOTE

Editing Tim Lloyd's letters has mainly been a matter of selection. I have omitted passages of purely family interest and some repetitions. I have also corrected Tim's erratic spelling and punctuation. He had a habit of emphasizing words in capital letters, and this I usually decided not to follow. By and large, however, there was little to be done, especially in the later letters.

Raleigh Trevelyan

Part One

Tim Lloyd died around midnight on 26 July, 1944, in the Arno Valley between Arezzo and Florence. He was aged twenty-two, a lieutenant in the Rifle Brigade. His letters in the second half of this book cover the period when he was in North Africa and Italy. In some ways they could be read as the kind of letters that a son facing an unknown future in war might write to a mother whom he deeply loved: reassuring, leaving out bits that might seem alarming – even though in Tim's case the actual time spent at the front was less than four weeks. What makes them special is his gift for describing landscape and people, moving counterparts to a personality seen by colleagues in the Army as blithe and courageous, even carefree.

Most of us have found ourselves thrown together for long periods with individuals whom we might not otherwise have met, because we were neighbours, at school together, perhaps, in the same office – or in the Army. Eventually we move on, the years pass, faces and even names are forgotten. Tim made such an impression on even fleeting acquaintances that memories of him have remained vivid after fifty years. The word 'gaiety' crops up frequently in letters from friends describing him. He had such an extraordinary zest for life, such a talent for enjoyment and appreciation of beautiful things. In those Army days, whenever we found ourselves somewhere totally boring, or were faced with what seemed hopelessly depressing conditions, he would immediately set about cheering us up, playing the fool if need be. I came across an obituary of Tim in a Rifle Brigade regimental history that seemed exactly right: 'He captivated everyone with his personal charm, infectious gaiety, and his untiring energy to get the best out of every possible situation, enjoying every minute of his so short a time on earth. He was a delightful companion, who had a circle of friends as wide, and as widely chosen, as few can boast, being interested in everything and everybody.' Children also loved him, as I found in the last months of his life in Italy.

At the time he was killed I regarded him as my best friend. I was then twenty-one, and had been keeping a diary. Only recently I re-read my account of his death, for the first time since I had written it, and found myself plunged into memories that I had hoped I had put to rest. In my mind then I had equated the circumstances of his being killed with some earlier experiences of my own. Did I really believe that I had actually seen it happen, or had it been a dream? Moonlight, dark shadows in a valley, a ruined building, figures emerging, a challenge, red darting flickers from a Schmeisser? I forced myself to look at earlier pages of that diary, at happier, and sometimes extravagant, times together: swimming with Renata and Vincenzina at Posillipo, posing with statues of Diana and Actaeon in the great fountain at Caserta, watching the sun set over Alger-le-blanc. Those things, and of course the jokes, were more like the Tim that I and others wanted to remember.

I first coincided with him at Fulford Barracks, York, towards the end of 1942. He and I were among the newly commissioned officers who were later sent to a dreary conglomeration of Nissen huts called Ranby Camp, near Retford. Tim had already been out in the world before going into the Army and seemed exotic and more sophisticated to us younger ones, who had joined up straight from school. He had a gramophone and a cocktail shaker in his room, which he shared with Mike King, a friend from his Repton school days, and which they called the Juke Box. It was much more amusing to be with them than in the stuffy

4

Officers' Mess. Most of our group met again at Philippeville in North Africa, and there the Juke Box was recreated. I got jaundice at Philippeville and Tim got diphtheria, so we were not able to join our friends on the draft to Italy. Eventually we found ourselves convalescing outside Algiers. It was then that our real friendship began. We had very little to do except to go to bars and clubs, and to make expeditions inland across the Atlas. All the same it was frustrating not being able to rejoin our regiment. Somehow accounts of casualties among friends and of the horrific conditions at the front made us all the more anxious to be off. Maybe we were feeling guilty, enjoying ourselves so much. But we were also afraid of being seconded to some 'brass button' regiment. In a silly snobbish way we had been brought up to believe that only the 'black button' Greenjackets – the Rifle Brigade and the 60th Rifles – were socially acceptable, apart of course from the Brigade of Guards and maybe two or three Cavalry regiments. We were, however, soon to find ourselves changing our minds.

Arriving at Naples was not at all what we expected. It was sheer desolation and misery: ships upside down in the bombed harbour, people begging, even snow. Not long afterwards Tim fell ill again, and I found myself in the trenches of Anzio. At one period I spent three weeks in a kind of cave under a cowshed that my platoon called Smoky Joe's (in a book I wrote I changed the name to Steamboat Bill's). It was almost impossible to put one's head out of that filthy hole during daylight without being sniped at. A letter from Tim was delivered to me one night, written in the special sort of language that we sometimes used. After reading it several times I wrote in my diary: 'He'd soon brighten us up here – only this place would be called the Juke Box, not Smoky Joe's, and instead of gooey Compot tea out of mess-tins we would have "sippikins" from his cocktail shaker. I have never known Toumi [my name for him] have blackers, and he never allowed anyone else to have them either. However gloom-making the circumstances – a cattle truck (*hommes 40: chevaux 8*) jogging through snow in the Little Atlas, a leaky tent near

Foggia, a Nissen hut full of hostile majors at Retford – he always had the answer: the Juke Box. Out came the cocktail shaker; garish Wog cushions were shaken up and fur-lined coats thrown in careless heaps; then Toumi would produce some miraculous drops of gin or cognac that somehow he'd managed to preserve, and he would mix it up with anything that had a taste, even toothpaste, provided it wasn't actually poisonous. Later, as we began to warm up, he would treat us to an exhibition of Ouëd Naïl belly dancing or one of Frances Day's latest numbers.'

In actual fact there were times in Algiers when we did feel fed up, I more so. He called it Algeriana. We also, I must admit, had one or two quarrels when this happened, but they were not serious.

Timothy Peter Lloyd was born on 22 March, 1922. His parents were Samuel Janson and Daisy (Margaret Ellen) Lloyd, who had married in 1896. He was the youngest of their thirteen children, two of whom had died young. The two eldest, Charles and Billy, were with good reason regarded as the difficult ones. The third was Priscilla, known as Pierre, who married W.A.R. (Billy) Collins, famous after the war in the literary world as Chairman of Collins the publishers. Then came Noey (Noel) who was killed in a crash with an American army vehicle soon after Tim's death, Pen (Philip Henry), David, Mary, Mike, Roo (Ruth) who was mentally retarded, and Kit (Christopher) who was killed at Dunkirk.

Pierre was highly strung, very religious, with considerable taste in décor and a feeling for literature. In some ways she was most like Tim. He especially loved her eldest daughter Deborah, four years younger than him. He adored Roo. He was also close to Kit, being the nearest in age and whom he called Blimpy. There was a marked family resemblance between most of the brothers and sisters: a rather pointed chin, fair wavy hair usually brushed straight back.

They lived at Pipewell Hall near Kettering, a large house, part of which has now been pulled down. Sam Lloyd (Pop) had been a director of the family iron and steel firm, Stewart and Lloyds, previously Lloyds Ironstone, at Corby. The Lloyds had been a Welsh Quaker family, moving to Birmingham as a persecuted minority in the 1690s. They became owners of ironworks and were among the earliest pioneers in country banking. They also promoted the Birmingham Canal. New ironstone workings were opened at Wednesbury, early in the nineteenth century, by three brothers of the senior branch. After a while the eldest brother, George, retired from the partnership in order to confine himself to the bank, which in 1865 became a limited liability company, the forerunner of the present Lloyds Bank. The two other brothers, Samuel – known as 'Quaker' Lloyd – and Sampson ran into financial trouble when they underestimated the cost of Blackfriars Bridge in London. 'Quaker' Lloyd's son, also a Samuel, started a tube-making firm at Wednesbury. He was Tim's grandfather. The story goes that this Samuel was passing near Corby in a train and noticed some red-coloured earth, which he knew meant iron. So he bought the land from Lady Cardigan, and that was the beginning of Stewart and Lloyds. The first iron came running out of the blast furnaces in 1910.

Tim's mother was née Philips. Her family came from Staffordshire. I met her three or four times after the war, when she was going blind. Roo was always with her, watching warily; if she knew you approved of her, she took you to her heart, and I think she approved of me. Mrs Lloyd, like Tim, and indeed like Pierre, whom I got to know well, was full of enthusiasms. She would go anywhere, I would be told, was game for anything. In the very cold winter of 1940 she played goal at ice hockey. Sometimes if she had rows with Pop she would sit on the stairs until all had cooled down. Deborah remembers her making tremendous flower arrangements and her ability to 'make things out of nothing' like stones. After the telegram had arrived about Tim's death her daughter-in-law Evadne, wife of David, went to her in the pantry. 'I shall be all right quite soon,' Mrs Lloyd said.

Pipewell was always full of people. The Collins family at first lived in part of it. Then there were relatives such as Humpo

Philips, almost an adopted son. Tim had a room in the attic, which he decorated in fantastic ways. He was regarded as being very good with his hands, and taught Deborah how to use a treadle fretsaw, and to sew and knit. He also taught Roo how to knit socks.

Kit was at Repton when Tim arrived there. The first letter from Tim to his mother was written on a half-holiday, and dated 30 June, 1936. He was hoping to play tennis. 'I am painting lampshades in Drawing at the moment, and have found a lovely place in a tree overhanging a bit of the old [River] Trent, where I cannot be seen but can see; it is just above a moorhen's nest. The eggs are not hatched yet. I can also see a water-rat's hole. It

was not at all a nice day yesterday. It rained a lot. We went to tea with the Bursar, and played clock golf in the evening. Nothing of interest has happened lately except Kit made 144 runs not out the other day in a House match. I like some of the masters, and *hate* some. There is McCattley, his father was a great enemy of Pop's when he was here, he is foul!! He takes us in Geography. I am always late for that. And then there is Dr Barton, the Science master; he is nasty too. Write again soon please. I am getting on quite well with the Art master, but he is so solemn, he never smiles at all. I hope you are all very well. Love from Tim.'

He created a marionette theatre at Pipewell during the holidays, and the sets and puppets became ever more elaborate. He put on a Coronation Revue in 1937, featuring Casanova and Ginger Rogers, then a Grand Christmas Pantomime, *Babes in the* Wood, with a highwayman and, rather oddly, Casanova once more. These would be accompanied by gramophone music, with bits taped over on records that he did not want to use. He took part in house plays at Repton, where, judging from a letter written after his death, he made a great impression on the headmaster, the Rev Michael Clarke. 'There were qualities he had which no other has shown,' Michael Clarke was to write. 'He was such a joyous creature, so unspotted. I suppose that it was his imagination that made him value things differently from everybody else. When one was with him, if one fell under his spell, as I did, the matter-of-fact point of view hardly counted, and life had to be thought of in terms of those values of his. I shall treasure so many exquisite memories of him, the soft shy voice in which he used to talk when he was serious, the way he used to open his eyes as a sign that he was moved, the fine sense of humour that underlay all his actions. It was over the acting that we came to know each other really well, and I shall never cease to rejoice at little things he did so deftly, either in the part he was playing, or in helping with productions, where he had something like genius.'

Michael Clarke took Tim on an expedition to Dovedale. 'He is *quite* different,' Tim wrote, 'when he is away from Repton. He even said to me about another master, "He has nothing to talk about except schools and school life." We walked up hills and saw the most wonderful views of the autumn colours and misty valleys.' He added (a great compliment), 'Dr Clarke is *very* appreciative'.

In 1937 Tim went to Vevey in Switzerland with his mother and Roo, his first trip abroad. Later they travelled to Bellagio and Stresa and climbed Monte Mottarone. In the following year he went to Davos. The Swiss scenery and the Italian lakes had an overwhelming effect on him, as if he had seen paradise. I often heard about these trips when we were at Algiers. To him going back to Italy was a vision of endlessly turquoise skies, campaniles, reflections of mountains and rhododendrons in the still waters of lakes. I suppose I had my fantasies about Italy too.

He started putting on marionette shows for friends and local Women's Institutes during the holidays. He would wear a pillbox hat for these. His favourite puppets were Frances Day and one called Sadie. These two were privileged to be taken to Repton, where Frances Day performed her numbers from the shows *The Fleet's Lit Up* and *Floodlight*. He then began to plan something much more elaborate: a puppet version of *The Mikado*, which was performed both at Repton and at Pipewell. He was allowed to design the sets in his Art classes at school, where he also studied architectural drawing. Members of his family – his mother, Deborah and Roo, among others – were not quite such proficient actors or singers, but he managed to keep his temper, and decided to take the main parts himself. His brothers evidently did not quite share his passion for the theatre.

He left Repton in April 1940, and his hair became suddenly blond. Evadne Longsdon came to stay at Pipewell. She was the daughter of Sir Archibald Flower, who had rebuilt the Memorial Theatre at Stratford-upon-Avon after the original theatre had been burnt down, and who had formed the first resident Shakespeare company. When she invited Tim to stay at Stratford for Shakespeare's birthday, he jumped at the chance. 'If you ask him to stay a week,' David said, 'he'll stay a year.' That nearly came to pass. (Evadne married David some years later.)

Tim was at Stratford when Kit was killed at Dunkirk. He returned for a while to Pipewell. Soon the younger actors at Stratford were being called up for military service. He had become friendly with an actress, Jean Byam, and it was partly thanks to her, but mainly through the influence of the Flower family, that he appeared in doublet and hose in *The Merry Wives of Windsor*. Lady Flower, ever more eccentric, used to send her car each night to fetch him after the show, in spite of petrol rationing. Jean and Tim (still blond) were revellers in *The Merchant of Venice* and both had parts in *Measure for Measure* and *She Stoops to Conquer*. Tim was a huntsman in *As You Like It*. The chief actor was usually Baliol Holloway. Thea Holme also had main parts. The producer was Iden Payne, and Tim was allowed to help with the sets.

Tim used to take Jean punting on the Avon. Lady Flower, who was Irish, born Florence Keane, became 'besotted' with him. He would be seen on the back seat of her car, while she in her turban sat in front. At night she would lock all the doors of the house and put the keys in the cold water jug in her bedroom, for the maid to fish out in the morning. The story goes that she once locked Tim in the lavatory and that he had to stay in there all night.

After the Stratford season of plays was over Tim went with his mother to Portmeirion in North Wales. He fell in love with this Italianate fantasy, 'like a beautiful stage set,' he later said, and longed to see the real thing in Italy. He was now considered to be totally wrapped up in the theatre. Jean, who was to marry Jack Flower, the second son of Sir Archibald and Lady Flower, continued to play in rep and eventually joined the WRNS. Tim took Evadne to the experimental Players Theatre, and she in turn introduced him to 'Cockie', C.B. Cochran, who suggested that he might try out his marionettes on Bob Lecardo of ENSA (Entertainments National Service Association), which Basil Dean had established under the aegis of NAAFI (Navy, Army and Air Force Institutes), the catering organization for the Forces. Already a group known as the Lanchester Marionettes, from Malvern, were touring the country in ENSA and proving popular.

Meanwhile Tim was planning another grand Christmas pantomime at Pipewell: *Dick Whittington*. His 'star' was Tilly Losch. This was followed by something much more ambitious: Hans Andersen's *The Sea Maid*, performed in aid of Beaverbrook's Spitfire Fund. It ran for a week, including matinées, and received good notices in the local press, useful for showing to Bob Lecardo. Mrs Lloyd, Deborah and Roo were kept busy serving teas.

All went well with ENSA. Tim was given a contract by NAAFI and a salary of £7 per week, first with the Suit Case Company and then, more grandly, with the Coliseum Variety Company. Sadie, Frances Day and Tilly Losch were joined by Bébé Daniels, Carroll Gibbons playing the piano, Evelyn Laye, Mae West and Colonel Bogey. Altogether Tim played in thirty-three theatres. His first letter to his mother in this period was from Magnolia Villas, Rhyl. That old trooper from music hall days, Nellie Wallace, was in his company and a bit of a trial. But 'she is all right if you pull her leg'. He complained of fleas and dirty blankets in his digs. 'Variety people never seem to wash!' 'The manager's wife has at least a week's make-up on and still her spots show through. And this house does not possess anywhere to wash

except in the kitchen, which is usually full of dirty children. I guess I am seeing life. The show went well this evening; nice theatre, holds about seven hundred. The usual back stage fights are in progress. Lots of love. I miss you like hell.'

At Chester he at least was able to have a bath. He became friends with the three acrobats in the company, called Tom, Dick and Harriette. 'They are very nice, they never have rows with anybody. Their family have been acrobats for six generations, though some are marionettists or Punch and Judy people.' They insisted that he should join them in a circus after the war. But, he said, his big friend was a Russian girl called Kyra Vayne. 'She speaks perfect English and has a wonderful voice, but unfortunately is always fighting with the other women.' Bob Lecardo had come to watch them work, and had been pleased with Tim's act.

In July, 1941, the time had come to register with the Army, though his call up papers would not be through until December. At Glasgow and Edinburgh they played to two hundred sailors a night – 'the best audiences in the world'. 'I have never enjoyed myself more because I felt they were really pleased to have us.' Kyra continued to be temperamental and said in Glasgow that she had 'lost all interest' in her voice. So Tim forced her to answer an advertisement in the *Stage* for a part in the chorus of Moussorgsky's comic opera *Sorotchintsi Fair*, to be performed at the Savoy Theatre in London on 6 October. Soon afterwards he was writing from Aldershot with the splendid news that she was to play the principal female part. 'This part is so big that she can only play it four times a week, because of the strain on her voice. So another woman [Oda Sblodskaya] is working for the other nights. I feel so proud. The opera includes a ballet, *Night on the Bare Mountain*.' And sure enough, she was a success. One paper, he said, even described her as the 'opera find of the century'. 'The audience would not let her go until she had made a speech and received ten bouquets of flowers. The next day she got forty telegrams of congratulations.

She really is a star now. Let's hope that some day I'll be the same.'*

Thanks to Kyra he was put in touch with George Kirsta, who had produced and designed *Sorotchintsi*. He had dinner with Kirsta and Evelyn Laye, about to star in *The Belle of New York*. 'I told her about my puppet of her, and she seemed quite flattered that anyone should take the trouble to make one.'

Tim joined the Rifle Brigade at their Winchester Depot. Immediately he wrote a quick note to his mother: ' "Just Dazed!" All goes well though. Life is very hard. Seventeen in bedroom, with "Billy the Boy's Double" sleeping six inches away. No room between beds. Most of the boys are from the East End or are road labourers. But I know I shall get used to it in time, as I did with ENSA. But I do wish I had someone of my type to talk to. I don't think I shall mind getting up at 6 a.m., because the beds are so hard. Thank you for your book of prayers, which is a great help. Love to all and don't worry.' In a very short time, and typically, he got himself organized. He had met a girl with whom he used to go skiing at Davos, and she had invited him to a dance. It had also leaked out at the Depot that he had been in ENSA, and he had given a show in the cinema. It was a terrific success, he wrote, and he had not only been asked to do another, but to compère a show that was to be broadcast from Luton. He had accepted this last, but his company commander had refused to let him go, saying that it would be bad policy, and the men would not like it. 'As a matter of fact they were *thrilled* and looked on me as something above everybody else, and *nothing* was too good for me. Perhaps that was why he would not let me do it. But even though it is unreasonable, and I miss one of the biggest chances I ever had, I am completely resigned to not making a fuss. This is the first time I have been strangled by red tape, and I am afraid not the last. My room mates said they were very proud of me. I have

* Kyra Vayne was to sing with Richard Tauber in *Gay Rosalinda* in 1945. She also was the first Leonora in *Trovatore* and the first Tosca in the Welsh National Opera. She sang Tosca at the Rome Opera in 1956.

had many offers for cabaret at dances here, and for children's parties, including the CO's! I don't know if I shall be allowed to do them or not.' He complained to his mother about army boots, especially as he had to go on twelve-mile 'route' marches at full speed. Since the Rifle Brigade was largely composed of Cockneys, who were very small, it was alleged to take shorter steps and a quicker pace than most other regiments. He had also been having to heave coal, affecting his hands which needed to be kept supple for the marionettes.

He went next to Tidworth in Hampshire, where there were even fewer comforts: 'as I expected all barracks and solders.' We have to apply for a pass three days before, if we want to go out, so I can't see myself being able to get away often.' 6923351 Rifleman Lloyd T.P. was living with thirty-two other men in a tin hut known as the Hen House, because of the two-tier bunks in a row down the centre. One boy couldn't read or write, and Tim had to compose his love-letters to his girl friend. 'The training is very much harder than at Winchester, but when treated decently I can put up with anything.' It was hardly worth Mrs Lloyd trying to come and see him. The consolation of Tidworth was the garrison theatre, where Tim had played in ENSA. The manager recognized him immediately and gave him the best seats, which Tim said sent him up in everybody's estimation.

He was worried about whether or not he would get a commission in the Rifle Brigade or be sent to another regiment. Strings were pulled, and at last he got into an OCTU (Officer Cadets Training Unit) at Perham Down. 'What a change. You have no idea what a difference it makes to have hot water, baths, spring beds (one spring) and food which is dished up instead of being thrown at you, and above all being called Sir by the sergeant-major and others. All the same, it is still a case of "Mr Lloyd, you are a bloody idiot, Sir".' Soon things were not so easy. His platoon sergeant had taken a 'diabolical dislike' to him, because he was applying for too many weekend passes to go to London. 'He has been telling lies that I could not prove to be untrue, and now he has succeeded in getting my passes stopped. I am very annoyed to think that my word could be doubted. We were to have a party in London last weekend, and as I was stopped I have to wire hectically to Christine [Mortimer Wheeler], who was coming up specially from the country, to put her off. A *great* factor is that being confined to barracks for a month means I am saving a lot of money.'

As soon as he was released from his confinement he was off to Queen Charlotte's Ball and sundry deb dances. Sometimes he stayed with Kyra. Then great news – he was to be transferred to the Greenjackets OCTU at York, which definitely meant the Rifle Brigade. He also wrote, perhaps significantly, because he was getting low in funds, 'It couldn't be better, miles and miles from London which is good, and a very pleasant town with lots to see.' But what he had not realized (and it was to dawn on me later in the year) was that, however chic it might be to join the Rifle Brigade, both Greenjackets regiments were composed of Motor Battalions. This meant that you had to be mechanically minded, able to drive Bren gun carriers and be proficient in mending wirelesses, as well as learning how to do things such as falling off a motor cycle without hurting yourself. Tim was not mechanically minded and failed on his wireless test – he 'couldn't get a grip' on the thing – and thus he was kept back for another two months before he received a commission. It was a severe blow to his social plans too, as he had been banking on the extra subaltern's pay. 'My CO [Dick Southby] was very nice about my wireless failure and explained that a subaltern in a Motor Battalion has to know as much as a captain in the infantry, so it was no disgrace to be put back. It is a bore, but I *shall* have very much more training, and will feel more confident as an officer when the time comes.'

Tim also added: 'I had a very nice letter from Deborah asking for a Rifle Brigade badge and a sample of the lavatory paper we use here!! The dirty little brute. I am sure Billy Collins would be shocked if he knew.'

Deborah, cross-questioned about this affair fifty-one years

later, has excused herself by saying that lavatory paper in those days used to have verses and jokes printed on it. 'Everyone else was collecting things, so I thought I would be different.'

Mrs Lloyd, realizing how disappointed he would be, came up to York for the weekend. They went rowing on the River Ouse.

This was the stage when I first met Tim. We of the new 'intake' were mostly aged nineteen. He was then twenty. From memory there must have been about eighty of us in the OCTU, some destined for commissions in the Rifle Brigade, some in the 60th Rifles, alternatively known as the KRRC, King's Royal Rifle Corps. We were divided alphabetically into two platoons, A–L and M–Z, thus sleeping in two different and very large barrack rooms. Tim was regarded by us as the 'full seasoned warrior', as he would put it, not to say a sometimes outrageous one. I see he said in a letter that many of his new companions were not Public School, which he found a relief. I had an introduction in York to a glamorous creature called Marigold Moule, half Australian, very tall with scarlet nails and golden hair, said to be only just seventeen. She told me that her smart girl friends were anxious to meet cadets (of the Public School variety), so I enlisted the help of Tim. Together we planned a party at the Station Hotel. Twenty boys and twenty girls sat in a circle in a private room drinking one glass of sherry each, which was all we could afford. It was a success, resulting in one marriage and three engagements (but which came to naught). Tim said he and I obviously had a future as pimps. We called Marigold 'La Belle Moule sans Merci', and were annoyed to hear that our colonel, Dick Southby, had taken her out. I don't think Tim was all that keen on the De Grey Rooms in York, where I used to like to go dancing. Trips to London were relatively rare because of the expense, and quite often we had to sleep in the guard's van on the way home among the rail bags.

Tim stoically endured a second round of 'toughening up' courses with the rest of us. 'Yesterday,' runs a letter, 'we did ten miles cross country in full equipment in two hours, as well as scaling a twelve-foot wall. There were bayonet practices, assault courses, plenty of PT.' Most arduous of all was the so-called Scheme on the Northumberland moors, which Tim rightly called Hell on Earth. It lasted a week. 'If anyone says the Army is soft, I shall kill them! We did a thirty-mile march across the mountains, sleeping in heather or anything else we could find. The march lasted two days, and we only had four sandwiches and eight biscuits for the whole thing, and had to carry forty pounds of equipment. Of course it just had to rain all week, so after the first day we and our bedding were soaking. After the march we did an exercise with real bullets. Lots of fun; I nearly shot two colonels and a general.'

One of those colonels was the always dapper Dick Southby. He had infuriated us by coming to inspect us at the very end of the Scheme, dressed in immaculately polished riding boots and carrying a swagger stick with a shiny silver knob, with which he prodded us. We of course by then were filthy and exhausted. I think we all would have liked to have a shot at him after that ordeal.

Those who were finally commissioned into the Rifle Brigade were sent to Ranby Camp and that included Tim and me. It also meant home for Christmas. 'Put out flags and kill at least one fatted calf!' Tim wrote to his mother.

I had been appalled by Ranby, which struck me as a hole in the middle of nowhere; the officers' quarters were on one side and all the rest on the other. Tim in his usual way made the best of it. 'This place is quite fantastic, so pompous and with hundreds of little traditions etc. (but quite fun) and strict etiquette in the mess.' He set about 'binging us up' in the Juke Box. Mike King, who shared it with him, looked so amazingly like Tim that we called them the Heavenly Twins. The puppet Sadie suddenly appeared and was put in a place of honour. We formed a kind of set, mostly from the new intakes: Nick Mosley, Charley Morpeth, Jimmy Stevens (who shared a platoon with me), Bubbles Nicholson, Eddie McGrigor, John Macalpine (known later as Mepacrine), Henry Hall and, especially, Zombie Wyndham-Green – nearly all of whom reappeared with us in

Italy. For a while we were joined by Egg Hallinan (otherwise the Egg), who had once been a monk. One or two of the less stuffy senior officers were sometimes admitted. These included Kit Barclay and Freddie Beausire. Then there was the incomparable Bunny Roger, a great friend of Tim's, and for that matter of us all, who kept us constantly laughing. His room was known as the Club Savoy, because he had a gramophone record which ran 'Boy, did I get stinking in the Club Savoy. Boy, did I go swinging on the chandeliers.'

Nick (Nicholas) Mosley in *Beyond the Pale* has written about the Juke Box – 'where we would indulge in some of the fantasies that seem often to be on the periphery of the consciousness of soldiers – among Greeks and Trojans, Shakespeare seems to suggest; apparently among – ah! – the Nazi SA. We would put music on and dance; one or two of us would dress up; we were Narcissi paddling among our own murky reflections. How innocent this was! – or is it innocent if soldiers manage the dirty business of war?' I confess I can't remember the dancing, but perhaps we did dance. Those rooms were very small and always crowded. I do say in my diary that we played 'silly games just to get away from the mess atmosphere'. Bunny has said that we played charades. Much depended on the energy we had left, after a hard day's training or route marches.

There were other diversions, of course, the Old Bell at Barnby Moor for instance. Occasionally we would take our platoons to pubs in Retford, and there were All Ranks Dances where we could flirt with ATS girls, and where we could also meet socially Riflemen who had been with us in the ranks at Winchester. Ranby was on the edge of the Dukeries, and soon invitations from 'top dogs', as Tim called them, would be forthcoming. The two nearest families with big houses were the Whitakers of Babworth Hall and the Darleys of Ranby Hall. The Whitakers were elderly and related to friends of mine, so I often went there for baths. Ranby Hall was much more frequented by everybody else, particularly as it had a squash court. Tim became a great favourite with the family, especially with the daughter, Deedie

Darley, whom he used to take to dances at Retford Town Hall. One weekend he managed to persuade his mother to come up and stay at the Old Bell, so she could get a glimpse of the 'horrors' of Ranby Camp.

Much of our training in driving lorries or Bren gun carriers was in the parks of Welbeck, Clumber and Thoresby, churning up the ground into seas of mud. Nearly every week we were off on schemes, sometimes for a couple of nights. For me the most memorable was in the idyllic country of the Peak District, under cloudless skies, where I played a ridiculous game of hide-and-seek with Nick Mosley's platoon, ambushing, and rushing into each other's camps, throwing thunder-flashes.

Tim's first platoon, he wrote, consisted of thirty men or 'lads' with eleven Bren gun carriers and sundry motor bikes. 'The "lads" range from 18 to 35 years of age and are a motley crowd, including a Chinaman, a negro and a sergeant from the Peruvian army.' Obviously these lads soon fell under his famous spell. 'They are very funny and we got on very well. They just couldn't *believe* that I was ever a rifleman too, until one of them met a man who had been with me in the ranks. He must have said that I was quite a good sort.' But soon there was trouble, and he wrote: 'Life has been *very tricky* here, my bloody NCOs have been absolutely hellish lately, fighting each other and having arguments before the men. Not that I care a damn about the NCOs, but the men notice that all is not as it should be, and of course that is disastrous. The climax came when I caught my corporal telling one of my men that if he didn't clean his motor bike he would ask me to stop his leave for six months. I was LIVID. Sparks flew in all directions, and the corporal is becoming a private in the near future, and is being posted to the Pioneer Corps. This of course caused a sensation, which makes for other dramas . . .' One of the dramas was to concern a new sergeant, 'a very stupid unintelligent bully, very much of the same type as the one I had at Perham Down'. 'I don't care, because the boys are keen as mustard and realize that I am "on the level". They come to me with their family problems and love affairs. I just don't have a moment to myself these days. At last I have found a job that suits and interests me.'

Looking back, I am surprised not only how often we were able to spend weekends in London, but how inexpensive it seems to have been to stay at the Savoy or the Berkeley, although there was also an officers' club at 101 Piccadilly where one could sleep at half a crown a night (and where now is the Japanese Embassy). London in the blackout, especially when there was a moon, had a special haunting beauty. Those birds may not have sung in Berkeley Square, but it was the centre of many romances. London was so silent too. Sirens came suddenly like mournful ghosts, and were part of that strange background. The possibility of danger from bombs made us determined to enjoy ourselves all the more. The fashionable restaurant was the Bagatelle, opposite the Mayfair Hotel, where one could dance between courses. It was also convenient to be able to take girls afterwards on foot from the Bagatelle to the Embassy nightclub in Old Bond Street. There we ordered full bottles of Gordon's gin, and were allowed to leave them unfinished, suitably marked with 'water-lines', until our next visit. Other night clubs, slightly further afield, were the Astor and the Four Hundred, the best and most expensive of all. If a girl was not likely to be shocked, she might be taken to the Nuthouse or even the Jamboree in Soho. At this last we danced on a glass floor with coloured lights underneath, and the cabaret was a striptease by a hot number called Pamela Saxby. A really perfect night out would end with breakfast in Lyons' Corner House in Coventry Street at 4 a.m., or even later.

We all affected to smoke Balkan Sobranie cigarettes, and most of us had our uniforms made at Sandon's in Savile Row. Mrs White in Burlington Gardens was the place for shirts. All this on a second lieutenant's pay. Once or twice I went with Tim to his favourite haunt, the Music Box, a drinking club off Shaftesbury Avenue. This was run by Muriel Belcher and Miss Dolly, Muriel being noted for pouring the larger drinks. Tim's particular friend was an old lesbian called Sod Johnson, whom he called Later Later Johnson. She used to follow us around to other dives, including the Ritz Bar, known then to some habitués as the Pink Loo. When the Music Box closed, Dolly married Alf Berger and they founded the Boeuf sur le Toit, and Muriel started up the Colony Room, which was to become famous. Tim never took me to these two last, presumably because he thought me too unsophisticated. But I was to hear a lot about them, especially the Boeuf, when I was with him in Algiers. He sometimes stayed at the Cavendish in Jermyn Street, but I was alarmed by stories of its proprietress Rosa Lewis, who was said to add the price of other people's champagne to your bill. I felt it was beyond my means. Some of our wealthier friends' mothers or aunts had permanent rooms in the Dorchester (being made of concrete it was supposed to be bomb proof) and, if we were lucky and they were away, we were allowed to sleep there.

A letter describes one hectic weekend. 'I got to London on Friday and had lunch with Charley Morpeth, Vivienne Mosley and her aunt. I then changed and went to a show with the Collins family. We had dinner at the Berkeley. Deborah was looking sweet in quite a grown-up dress and red finger nails!! It seems odd that only a short time ago she would take *no* trouble with her appearance. We danced afterwards. The next day I took the train to Eton with Nick and Viv Mosley, and who do you think was on it? The beautiful Prue [Stewart-Wilson], Deborah's friend! I have very much fallen for her. Also her brother is in the Rifle Brigade, which makes a big difference. I saw a lot of her during the day. At Eton I met a lot of friends, and in the afternoon we had a picnic on the cricket field, where we danced to a gramophone. We took Prue and Carol Macmillan to the Bagatelle and afterwards to the Four Hundred.'

Although not mentioned, I was in that picnic party. It was an enchanted, dotty afternoon. And I was to hear much of the 'beautiful Prue' thereafter.

Tim had a very expensive-looking khaki overcoat made at Sandon's, with a collar that buttoned right up to the neck and no belt. He said that he couldn't bear to wear the ordinary Army issue overcoat. I was very impressed, but couldn't afford to copy him. Instead I got a Retford tailor to shorten my Army overcoat and to take in the waist. I wore it a couple of times. It was not very comfortable. Then the Adjutant summoned me, and ticked me off. Soon afterwards I was transferred back to the Depot at York. I felt it was a disgrace, perhaps wrongly, but came quite to enjoy the job, which was training new recruits. It also meant that I hardly saw Tim for the next five months. I assume that he continued to wear his overcoat, without adverse comment.

His father died on 8 September. Tim was able to be at Pipewell then. A month later he got leave to take his mother and Roo to Portmeirion for a week. I was to have joined him on the draft abroad in November, but my departure was delayed by a few days so that I could see my father, who was returning from India after four years. Nick, Charley, Bubbles, Zombie and Bunny had already left. Our destinations were of course always secret, but it was assumed that they would be somewhere around the Mediterranean.

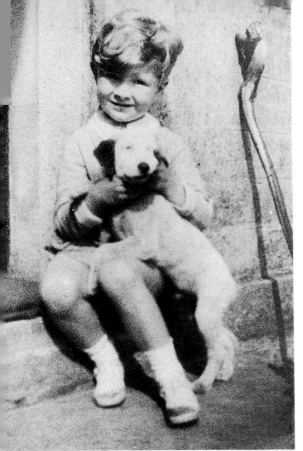

1. Tim aged two at Pipewell.

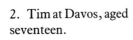

2. Tim at Davos, aged seventeen.

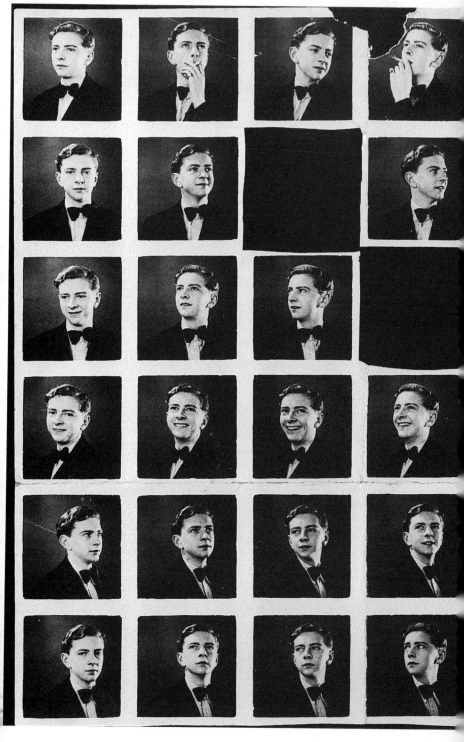

3. Tim aged eighteen; taken for ENSA, 1940

4. "He created a marionette theatre at Pipewell during the holidays" (p.8). Tim is seen here with 'Carroll Gibbons at the Savoy'.

5. "His favourite puppets were Frances Day and one called Sadie" (p.10). This is Frances Day.

6. Two pages from Tim's marionettes note b

riety Act.

THE SUIT CASE THEATRE

Troop Concerts for the AA + AAF Associations

ENSA ACT.

THE ALL STAR COMPANY

Bebe Daniels
Evelyn Laye.
Carroll Gibbons.
Frances Day.
Mae West.
Col Bogey.
Joe the Xylophonist

7. Tim's first stripe.

8. Raleigh Trevelyan on a 'scheme' in Yorkshire.

9. "Then there was the incomparable Bunny Roger" (p.19). Tim with Bunny at the window of the 'Juke Box'.

10. Friends at Ranby Camp, with the formidable Colour Sergeant Knights. Left to right: Henry Hall, John Bally, Dennis Matthews, Pat Cowan, Peter Beazley, Nicholas Mosley, John Macalpine, Desmond Nicholson, James Caesar.

11. Tim with two pips, on embarkation leave, October, 1943.

12. Tim's photograph beside his mother's bed.

13. Tim's mother, Margaret Ellen Lloyd.

Part Two

Tim's first letter after setting sail was in the form of a 'report' for general family consumption. He does not say so, but it seems likely that he was on an American ship, as I was to be a few days later. 'Turkey and unlimited butter' were unheard-of luxuries in 1943, not to mention things like chewing-gum and after-shave lotion.

GOING ABROAD (WARTIME EDITION)
by Lieut T.P. Lloyd

Having made a somewhat spectacular exit from Ranby Camp in the early hours of Armistice Day, 1943, with the band playing and the Colonel [Vic Turner VC] waving a red handkerchief, we were swished by private train to an unknown destination. Many thoughts passed through my mind, mainly of home, but it was thrilling wondering where we were going and what the boat would be like . . .

After several hours going north we arrived at our port of embarkation which, until the war is over, must be known as X [it was Liverpool]. X has a very imposing waterfront with high buildings and wide piers, not unlike a miniature New York. We were ushered on board without delay, and not allowed on shore again. Having settled into my cabin, which was 12 ft by 12 ft and containing seven other people, I went on deck to find a small group of very pretty FANYs [First Aid Nursing Yeomanry]. One was saying in a very Mayfair voice, 'Darlings, what a *divine* ship, just like a floating Claridge's!'

I couldn't believe my ears. Just then they were marched briskly away, leaving one poor unfortunate girl struggling with a huge kitbag. I saw my chance and rushed forward to help her with it. She was very sweet and most grateful, and explained that she was doing 'porter' for the day. I said goodbye and hoped I would see more of her. On my way back to my cabin I had another shock. Walking towards me was Johnnie Durst, one of my greatest Reptonian friends, who was going to make a film of AMGOT [Allied Military Government Occupied Territories]! He told me that Stanley Haynes, who had made 'Goodbye Mr Chips' at Repton, was on board, also Peter Ustinov, who is one of the most brilliant of England's coming playwrights. A very successful beginning to my trip.

We left X at sundown that night. What a wonderful sight it was, the black buildings silhouetted against the blood-red sky. After dinner, which consisted of four courses, including roast turkey and unlimited butter, I went on deck and watched the moon on the water.... I didn't feel I was losing anything by leaving England, but rather that I was gaining a lot by seeing new things and meeting new people.

Next day I went up on deck again to find that we were anchored about a mile from the coast, with mountains in the distance [in fact Snowdonia]. I was looking through my field glasses when a voice behind me said, 'Hello, I do want to thank you for carrying my kitbag yesterday.' It was the little blonde FANY who I had met the night before. After a few minutes of 'weather' talk, she said, 'Do you know if someone in your regiment called Tim Lloyd is on the boat? Some friends of mine in London said he was going abroad, and I thought he might be with you!' We have been fast friends ever since.

After a day or two we sailed [this time northwards], following the coast, until we passed Grey Gables [his clue to their whereabouts, Grey Gables being the Collins family home in Ayrshire], and eventually we arrived at Q, which must also remain nameless. Q [it was Greenock] reminded me a little of Fleilen on Lake Lucerne, little white houses with snow mountains in the background. At night it was quite lovely, all the shops had lights that looked orange in the white moonlight. We stayed only for two days and one night, and then one morning the convoy sailed away, leaving Britain behind us. Out at sea it was Up and Down, Up and Down, blustery wind and people being sick over the wrong side. What a performance. We ran a sweepstake on who would be sick first. If the person whose name was on your ticket was sick first you won the prize! Luckily the bad weather did not last long.

The FANY was called Diana ('Dipsy') Portman. She was travelling with her great friend Sue Ryder, now Lady Ryder of Warsaw, who has written of the journey in her book *Child of My Love*. The girls were doing top secret work in SOE [Special Operations Executive] connected with the Polish and Yugoslav Resistance, and were under oath to keep silent about it. Sue Ryder describes how they were asked awkward questions on board by officers in the Rifle Brigade. 'Our cover stories must have sounded very weak.' In her museum at Cavendish in Suffolk she has on display her Sam Browne belt signed by Peter Ustinov, Eddie McGrigor and Tim, who has written 'Just not of this generation' with a drawing of a girl in a crinoline and with a parasol – meaning of course that Sue was just the opposite to that type.

Sue also mentions the overcrowding of the troops below decks, some sleeping on the stairs. There was a tremendous feeling of boredom, she says, 'broken only by regular boat drills and occasional enemy attacks on the convoy'. Three ships were lost, but Tim naturally avoided this in his letter to his mother.

(undated)

Darling Mummie,
    I hope all goes well with you – I can tell you very little about my journey as censorship is very strict. Once again I must say that the food is good – too good to be true. I am just filling myself with butter and eggs. Unlimited supplies of both.
    My last letter may not get through, so in case it does not I will tell you again that we passed Grey Gables twice before leaving England – also we very nearly saw the place where you, Roo and I stayed in October [Portmeirion]. Quite a Cook's tour!
    The great thing about this trip is that I have had plenty of time to think and get things straight in my mind, and also to realize how much I have enjoyed the past few years, and

above all how much they have taught me. I can look back now, and think of the wonderful times I have had: Pipewell, Repton, ENSA, the army. All of them have something that is worth keeping and holding like a favourite book, which one can open and read when one feels like it. The funny thing is that I don't yearn to have those times back again, because there is so much hope for the future and for something that may be equally good, if not quite so comfortable. Whatever happens now will only be another chapter, and may be one of the most important – because for the first time in my life I cannot just telephone to you or one of the family and ask for advice. I must think and act by myself. But the advice you have given me in the past, and the understanding we have, will help no end. Your love means more to me than almost anything else, because you have always trusted me and believed in me, and I hope I have never, and will never, let you down. Last of all, however far away you are in fact, I can feel you very near and I always will be able to.

This is what I feel, rather badly put I am afraid, but I think you will understand.

All my love, Tim.

P.S. Lovely sunshine.

They disembarked at Algiers. Tim explored the Casbah, and was thrilled. It was like the Arabian Nights, he said. He was camped on the Race Course. He also lost no time in seeking out the right contacts, and called on Harold Macmillan, being a family friend, though the interview must have been short, Macmillan being just back from Cairo and preparing to meet that formidable Russian, Andrei Vyshinsky.

November 30th, 1943

I hope you have received my various airgraphs and letters. I am still in North Africa, and am more or less finding my feet. Life is so different here that one has to have one's wits about one the whole time. The thieving is quite appalling; nothing can be left unwatched for a moment. The Arabs steal complete officers' kits and sell them on the Black Market, which is highly organized here. There is no set price for the goods that one buys in the town, you just have to bargain for everything. Food is very expensive, and to get a good meal at a restaurant you have to spend £3! Anywhere cheap is just plain suicide, as the dirt and diseases are very dangerous.

The condition of the Arab quarter is unbelievable, filthy children men and women dressed in rags, crouching in the streams of dirt that run down the narrow streets. How human beings can exist in places like these, I do not know. Murder is a very ordinary occurrence.

In spite of all the sordid side of North Africa, I love the amazing buildings and the wonderful sunshine. The blue sea is the blue you tried to show me in Italy, and sunsets are quite the most beautiful I have ever seen. I sat in a little café on the waterfront last night and watched the sun set through a grove of brilliant red flowers, palm trees and cactus. I wouldn't have missed this for the world, and the marvellous thing is that there are nice people to enjoy it with.

By the way I am sending you some lemons and oranges. They should reach you about the New Year – and are quite green now, so will be ripe when they reach you. Could you send me some cigarettes as they are short here. You can send them duty free from a shop in Piccadilly . . .

I wish you could fly out here! I know a little villa that would just do for you; maybe we can have it after the war. The FANYs we met on the boat coming over are still with us. They couldn't be more charming, so we are not lonely! . . .

Must stop now – all my love and good wishes for Christmas.

Tim. Written without any clothes on, in blazing sun.

I too was in due course to find myself in that camp on the Race Course. We had actually to sleep on our kit, as Arabs would manage to creep past the guards and into our tents, stealing things while we slept.

(undated)

Here we are on the move again – but this time in a cattle truck, coupled to a very antiquated French train. We left yesterday, and ever since have been passing through the most impressive country. Yesterday it was very like a Cézanne picture, green sunlit hills with little white farms among the vineyard terraces. Arab farmers with their oxen and donkeys all dressed in the most picturesque cloaks and head-dresses. When we stopped, they rushed towards the train to sell us eggs, oranges, grapefruits, nuts and skins of wine. Just before dark last night, we stopped near an Arab village, it was wonderful. Processions of farm workers on donkeys and goats winding down the hill side, and all meeting in a tented encampment, where fires were burning and the evening meal was being prepared. The noise of chattering and bargaining was terrific, as they sold each other the produce of the day. The Arabs up in the hills are much nicer than the ones in the towns, not nearly so dirty and much more honest. After dark last night it was freezing, after a marvellous hot day. I put on David's flying suit, and it was a blessing because we had to sleep in our clothes with only one blanket.

Today we are going across a huge plain with very sandy soil and mountains on both sides. No houses at the moment, only a few mud huts and striped tents. The Arabs once again came running across the fields, but this time to buy food and clothes off us! One was last seen tearing away like a maniac down a deep gorge dragging an army blanket and a kitbag behind him, which he had pinched off the train; we hadn't time to go after him, so he got away. They try to buy things from the men, so we have quite a time trying to stop them.

6th December

We have arrived at a lovely place by the sea – plenty of good food and sunshine. The sea is the blue that you said it would be, so I must apologize for doubting it. I am sitting on the beach at the moment in a bathing costume gazing at a wonderful panorama of rocks, mountains, and a white town climbing up the hillside. What a beautiful place. I am loving every minute of it, in spite of the fact that I may not be sent to the Rifle Bde. Once again this 'other regiment' business has started, but I am not worrying too much about it, because things usually turn out alright in the end.

I hope this letter gets to you by Christmas. I would love to be with you, but it just can't be, so I shall think of you instead.

Lots of love and write soon, Tim

He was now at Philippeville, where there was a large Army Camp a few miles outside, up in the hills. Somehow, although I had arrived in North Africa after Tim, I had preceded him at Philippeville. 'Yah, White Knees,' Nick Mosley had greeted me. We were under canvas. The large communal latrines were particularly trying. 'I *must* tell my brother about these,' Tim said to me: a remark I thought peculiar at the time, but now on reading one of his later letters I understand why he said it.

He had at once discovered that Peter Ustinov and Carol Reed were at Philippeville, preparing to make a propaganda film called *The Way Ahead*. It was a pretty little town, hardly spoilt by the war. Thanks to the film people we were introduced to a once glamorous restaurant-cum-nightclub on the beach, where the food was still good and French, and where Tim said the head waiter looked like Humphrey Bogart gone to seed. The problem always was how to hitchhike back to camp. The roads were narrow and winding, dangerous in the dark, so one had to find a vehicle driven by someone who was not too drunk.

A group of us was conscripted to 'act' in a battle scene for *The Way Ahead*. We had to charge through smoke with fixed bayonets and looking belligerent. Otherwise we were kept busy with Schemes and on the shooting range. Once a Scheme took us through tangerine groves, and that was particularly enjoyable. Undeterred by notices such as *Attention – Pièges aux Hommes* we gorged ourselves on the fruit and filled our pockets. In fact the French farmers seemed not to mind, and gave some of us bottles of wine, which we enjoyed later at the recreated Juke Box.

I confess I am a little baffled by some of Tim's next letter, and cannot understand why he should have gone travelling here and there, and in so short a time, when the rest of us were perforce static, waiting to be despatched to Italy without notice.

(undated)

Once again I am comfortably installed in a cattle truck marked 'Hommes 40: Chevaux 8'. It is amazing how comfortable it can be in a cattle truck if it is your home for five days. What with David's flying suit, your sleeping bag and the picnic set I bought with Pierre's money, I might be in a suite at Claridge's. In fact Claridge's has been inscribed on the outside door by my batman.

I have seen so much lately that it is hard to know where to begin; anyway I have been to Algiers, Constantine, Tunis, Bizerta etc. Constantine is lovely, built on two hills, rather like Sion, but much larger and more spread out. Huge bridges span the gully and there are twin mosques on the hills. I want to spend some time there soon.

How wonderfully vague these railways are. You can never tell when you will get to your destination, because you may just stop on the line for about twelve hours, or leave half the train behind, and have to go back for it! When nature calls, you just hop off, do what you will, then run on and catch the train again. One man did this, and before he caught the train up again, it went into a tunnel, so he was left behind. No one minded, he just caught another the next day. The train I caught this time was only ten hours late; this was wonderful, as most trains are overdue by about three days – and to think how in England people grumble if a train is a quarter of an hour late.

We had a lecture the other day, and the man said that there was no chance of us going to the Rifle Brigade. I am pulling strings madly to get an outside job until things settle down a bit, because they *must* want us sooner or later. But it is a bit rough having been picked and sent out especially to join the Regiment.

Rattle, rattle, bump, bump, CRASH goes the truck, SCREAM goes the engine; the noise is deafening and we are still only going 10 miles per hour. V. stupid man opposite me, keeps complaining that the floor is hard, rather obvious I would have thought. My men have tied a brazier to the back of the train and are sitting on the buffers cooking a stew of bully beef, rice, carrots, army biscuits, eggs, and anything else that may be in reach; rather like a Pipewell hash.

The mail out here seems to be very erratic as I have had no letters at all yet. I am afraid a lot of them will get lost. I have tried to get some silk stockings for Debs.

All my love to everyone. Look after yourself. I will. Tim.

20th December

Once again in a train. I seem to spend my life on the rails. Have just spent a week in Algiers. It really is a lovely place, quite warm considering it is winter. I dined one night at a tiny café about five miles out with a lovely balcony overlooking the sea. A full moon silhouetting the palm trees and tropical creepers, the pink silk table lamps throwing a soft light over the whole scene. What could be nicer?

The next day I went right up into the mountains in a truck. The change of scenery was amazing. Snow, freezing cold and then a little village which should have been in Switzerland. A few châlets, a church with a pointed spire, and people skiing. Unfortunately, I hadn't time to ski, but I hope to go back there for longer in the near future. How I wish you could be here to enjoy these things too.

Am not having quite such a good journey this time, rather erratic. Last night at 11 p.m. I was turned out of the train at a tiny wayside station and was told that there would be no more trains until morning. So off I went with all my luggage to the waiting room, which to my dismay was full of Arabs. I found a corner and sat myself down on my suitcase and collected all my small things round me to stop them being pinched. This wasn't too bad for an hour, but after a while, the smell of garlic, bodies and other things was too much. The last straw was when an Arab spat, missed the floor and hit me! I belched in a gentlemanly manner, picked up my luggage and spent the rest of the night in blissful comfort on the platform in David's flying suit.

David's flying suit is a godsend. I can't think what I would do without it. It is so wonderful to be able to settle down *anywhere* and still be warm – please thank him accordingly.

(continuation of letter follows)

31st December

Too stupid I lost this letter and thought I had posted it.

I had a very pleasant Christmas with lots of good food etc., also lovely carol service with the Welsh Guards choir. Several new people have arrived, and I have seen Charley Morpeth who is trying to get me to his Battalion, the 10th [Rifle Brigade]. If this falls through I may try to transfer to the [deleted by censor] which is possible, I hear, anyway no [censored] at the moment.

By the way, I am in hospital at the moment with a very mild diphtheria. I don't mind in the least as six others from the Regiment are here too, and the rainy season is in full swing, so we are not missing anything. The beds are comfortable, the food good and the nurses divine!

I don't know how long I will be in, but they pumped me full of dope the first day, and it seems to have killed all the germs and not me yet, so that is satisfactory. We are allowed to sit up and walk to 'the loo', so as you can see there is very little wrong, and anyway I do love being in bed.

We have had no mail from home yet, which is a bore, but just keep on writing and some are sure to get through. I hope my letters are coming through alright.

All my love, Tim

It does now indeed seem odd that the military authorities should have been prepared to despatch us haphazardly in civilian trains. By this time I had contracted a form of jaundice, and was in fact for a while in the same hospital as Tim, though we were not allowed to meet. It had been a TB hospital, and was at Oued-Athménia, near Constantine. Being very high up, we were often under snow. On 6 January I was discharged, and having been told that the Philippeville camp had been closed down I, with eight Other Ranks, was duly launched out on a thirty-hour train trip to Algiers, luckily not in a cattle truck, but in crowded coach compartments, which made the problem of guarding one's kit all the more alarming.

Tim meanwhile had been sent to another hospital on the coast, perhaps at Bougie.

7th January, 1944

Sorry for this long gap in my correspondence, but with this bloody diphtheria one has to lie on one's back the whole time, and I can't write sense upside down. I am up and out of bed again now, and hope to be discharged within a few days. The weather has been quite awful here, RAIN, RAIN, RAIN. Last night there was a big storm and my tent blew down! You see, we are only 200 yards from the sea, and all the wind catches us. It is lovely this morning, sunshine again, and great breakers washing over the coast road right up to the edge of the hospital.

My first letters have just arrived, you can't imagine what it means. The post is so bad. Nearly two months of wondering what was going on at home. . . . Give Roo my love and tell her that I can't find any picture postcards for her out here, but that I have sent some pictures of Algiers inside a box of almonds I sent you a few weeks ago. Today I was moved into a villa on the sea shore called 'La Belle Maison', it couldn't be sweeter. My room has french windows on to a balcony verandah, with Moorish arches and looks over a garden of cactus and yellow mimosa to the sea. . . .

I must stop. It is heaven to see your writing again.

All my love, Tim

8th January, 1944

I went out today for the first time and sat on my verandah in the sun. . . . Glorious sunset tonight. A riot of colour. As the sun sank in the sky the huge sandstone rocks on the headland opposite my verandah turned to gold. Everything seemed to be touched with a golden brush, even the crests of the waves were tinged with pink, riding on the cornflower blue sea, finally crashing to a thousand sparkling particles on the rocky beach. The colours were wonderfully soft except the blue shadows of the palm trees on the white steps in front of me. As the dying sun dropped behind the mountains, it seemed as if a pale blue gauze had been dropped over the whole scene. Only the sky remained pink and the rugged mountains stood in black peaks silhouetted against the sky in every tone of red. Quite suddenly the air became bitterly cold, and I could wait no longer, but oh how beautiful it was.

Diana Portman (the FANY I met on the ship), came to see me today, a very pleasant surprise. The poor thing has just been on a three-day train journey. She travelled with 15 other girls in a cattle truck that was full of coal dust and smelt of horses! She was quite cheerful and said that never again would she pay double fare to go 1st class in England. It is amazing to think that girls of 19 and 20 can stand up to the strain of that kind of life after their so-called 'soft' upbringing. Incidentally she has been cooking for forty people on two oil stoves for the past fortnight, and sleeping in a double bed with two other girls. Such a flimsy and degenerate generation aren't we?

I keep on reading your two letters over and over again and longing for more.

All my love, Tim

14th January, 1944

Left hospital today and am once again on the train, doing the same three-day journey that I have done four times before. The sun is lovely today, but it is much colder and there is snow on the mountains which we have to pass through tonight. So I am afraid

T. LLOYD. 100th GENERAL HOSPITAL BNAF
VIEW FROM VERANDAH" JAN 8th '44
"LA BELLE MAISON"

it will be icy after the comfort of hospital. No lovely cattle truck this time, just a bloody 3rd class carriage which is creeping with bugs! Thank God I have been inoculated for typhus, because if I am not lousy by the end of this journey it will be a miracle!

Have come to the conclusion that some people will never enjoy beautiful scenery. Heard when we were passing through some of the most wonderful mountains I have ever seen:

Lt Snook: 'God, look at that, if there was a tank on that road, we could blow it to hell from here!', and 'Rather like Salisbury Plain isn't it?'

That I thought was rather like Roo comparing the Lion of Lucerne to Kettering War Memorial!

Have just got your letter about Christmas, I am so pleased it was a success. So wish I could have been there. Have you got the oranges, lemons, raisins, almonds etc. yet? I hope they haven't all got stolen in the post. All my love Mummsie darling, will write again soon, Tim

18th January, 1944

Here I am at rest again. This time in the most perfect little fishing village. I have been so lucky, my servant who is a Guardsman and speaks much better French than me, has found a room for us over a café on the water's edge. It is glorious, overlooking the harbour full of fishing boats with red tan sails, and a background of white houses and blue mountains. Raleigh Trevelyan and myself share it, and there is a very plump Madame who brings coffee and rolls in the morning and does our washing. I am afraid we won't stay here long, but anyway it *is* heaven while it lasts. I am feeling quite well again now, and there have been no diphtheria after effects, so that also is satisfactory. We went fishing yesterday evening and caught a very strange pink fish about a foot in length. It was quite rough, and Raleigh was sick over the side. The fish came rushing and I scooped them out with a net, mostly sardines but there were a few flat fish.

Leslie Henson is out here with a show: it is quite excellent, and of course very much appreciated. They are doing a week at the Opera in Algiers and a few odd shows around the camp. . . .

I am going up into the mountains tomorrow, as it is my day off. I think there will be snow. Tonight the sunset, from my café, was quite lovely, black silhouettes of the sails against a pink sky, and tiny white clouds round the mountain-tops. It is such a blessing to have all these wonderful things, even though one can't tell what the future holds in store. I will always be able to count this winter with the other times that I have enjoyed abroad in peacetime.

I sent some more dates and things today, and some 'Tres Chick Tres Snobb' French rope shoes to Deborah, the very latest from Mme De Gaulle's shoe shop. I am sure they won't be the right size, but anyway they will be fun to show to her girl-friends.

All my love Mummsie darling. Look after yourself. I will. God bless you. Tim

The fishing village was called La Pérouse, on the bay directly opposite Algiers. We were in a combination of training camp and convalescent home that also included a detention centre for some five hundred 'bomb-happies', men whose nerve had cracked in action and who in some cases had deserted. Some of our Rifle Brigade companions from York and Ranby days, recuperating from wounds in Italy, were also there, but none we considered particularly congenial. Perhaps that was why they called us Tatler and Bystander. From them we learnt that the 10 RBs – the 10th Battalion of the Rifle Brigade – were still in Tunisia, but unlikely to go to Italy for some months. Thus, whenever the time came to be transferred to Italy, it would inevitably mean being sent to a 'brass button' regiment.

At first there was very little to do at La Pérouse. As we were still officially convalescing, we took spells as duty officers, rather frightening on Friday nights – pay nights – when the whole camp was filled with shouting and singing, men collapsing in corners, pissing and being sick. Not, I knew, that I could really criticize, after so many hectic nights in Algiers. Any contact with the bomb-happies was liable to be distressing. Some were in a state of collapse, some belligerent and snarling like zoo animals. The compound officer horrified us: 'Treat 'em rough. That's all they understand. A good clout with the truncheon.' In due course we began training again and went on long route marches.

TO:- Mrs S. J. LLOYD.
PIDEWELL HALL
KETTERING.
ENGLAND. NORTHANTS

Lloyd.

Write the message very plainly below this line.

Darling
Mummy.

This is
a very
quick
Sketch
That I
managed
to make
from the
CASBAH
in
ALGIERS.
sometimes
hope all
goes well
with you.
love to
all
Tim

This space should not be used.

41

I had already paid frequent visits to Algiers, about six miles away, and used to sit in the cafés and drink at the Aletti Hotel, where there was an officers' club. When Tim arrived at La Pérouse life changed dramatically. Not only did I find myself being introduced to ENSA stars like Hermione Baddeley, Leslie Henson and Madge Elliott (off to play in *The Merry Widow* in Cairo), but Tim from his previous visits knew all the *louche* joints such as the Sphinx in the Casbah, strictly out of bounds to military personnel and where there was an unprintable *'exhibition'*. Our favourite haunt (not in the Casbah) became the Bosphore in Rue Tanger – 'terribly bogus, so corny, so hopelessly shoddy', I wrote in my diary, 'but wonderful'. There, amid 'all the smart Wog trappings' we watched what was billed outside as a 'brilliant floor show with swing orchestra', but described by me as consisting of 'skinny cabaret girls in tatty tights, great fat buses singing in "English", and performing dogs'. We drank

lots of mousseux out of earthenware jugs and a concoction called Hibbert's cocktail. Nobody had told me that I should not drink alcohol after jaundice, but it didn't seem to matter. Tim taught me how to make an entrance. He said that as we appeared at the door of the Bosphore everyone should look round and wonder who we were.

We also spent a lot of time looking for presents for Deborah and Roo. Those 'Tres Chick' shoes had thick rope soles, which I now learn Deborah did try to wear. Reading my letters home of that period, I wonder what my parents thought I was up to. The problem on those evenings out in Algiers was the usual one of finding a hitch back to camp after curfew. The road was said to be dangerous, and there were stories of knifings in the dark. As a last resort we would stay near the docks at the Wagons-Lits, which had been turned into a peculiar sort of transit camp.

We were both bowled over by Alger-le-blanc, as a book I had bought called *Mysterious Islam Life* described it. Somehow we managed to sneak into the Casbah by daylight. The women – with the 'most beautiful eyes in the world', according to that book – were all shrouded in white, as if bound for the morgue, Tim said. I wrote: 'There is a wonder at every corner – weavers, cobblers, tiny children darting here and there, beggar musicians with their wailing songs, vividly coloured blankets hanging in the shops. The noise, the filth. Oh it's thrilling. The guidebook says, "You may safely walk in these old corsairs' nests and admire their beauty." Admire their beauty, yes, but safely – ?!!' I also began to appreciate Tim's way with children. He had two pet shoeshine boys, Alouet and Hussein, who would never allow his shoes to be cleaned by anyone else.

Tim had several favourite words or catch-phrases. Now I can only remember a few. 'Get the gaiety of that!' was one, usually in an ironic sense. The word 'full' was another, meaning very, absolutely or complete, such as 'the full seasoned warrior' which I have already mentioned. He was fond of putting the word Rose before names, again ironically, especially if the person was a bit of a bore or rather mad. Sometimes he even referred to himself in the third person as Rose.

We moved into a tent which Tim at once converted into the Juke Box. He had bought some 'Bedouin' cushion covers which we stuffed with clothes and piled up haphazardly. His brother David's flying suit, sheepskin lining upwards, was left as if carelessly on a camp bed. A spiky leaved cactus was stuck in an earthenware jar with two handles. I had bought an Arab lute made from a tortoise's shell lined with goatskin, and that was put on view, until it began to stink. And of course the famous cocktail shaker was produced. We gave parties, with Tim's special 'sippikins', cocktails mixed this time with mousseux, a drop of cognac and orange juice. There was a special party when we heard of the landings at Anzio.

Over a hedge of prickly pears we could see from our tent the tiled roofs and minarets of the village. Beyond was the blue range of mountains above Algiers in the shape of a sleeping woman. When funds were low we were quite happy to stay quietly at La Pérouse.

26th January, 1944

Still in our little fishing village, with its café and quay. Sat on the beach all the afternoon fishing off the rocks, lovely sunshine the whole time. They have the most peculiar fishing boats here with two sails and two masts.

 I have tried to draw one on the left with little success. They are manned mostly by Arabs with white nightshirts and red skull caps. Delightfully colourful against the blue sea.

The countryside around here has quite suddenly become covered with wild flowers. Clumps of white michaelmas daisies growing wild on the hillside, and the vineyards are covered with marigolds and a sort of light yellow cowslip. The wild iris come in about a month, but the mimosa and pink and white almond blossom are in full bloom. Spring has come; even here there is that certain smell in the air that always reminds one of daffodils and narcissi.

The streets of Algiers are full of native vendors with baskets of spring flowers as well as roses, gladioli, and carnations. You can imagine how wonderful they look against the white buildings in the sunlight.

Yesterday I was lucky enough to get a truck which I took to Notre Dame d'Afrique, the largest church in North Africa. It stands on a rocky pinnacle high above Algiers. It is built in Moroccan style with dome, minarets etc., and is used by all religions; Catholics, Church of England, Moslem, and any other creed you can name – in fact a common place of worship for all North African peoples.

We left Algiers simmering in the heat of the afternoon and climbed away from the noise and hurly-burly of the town, until at last we arrived at the top of the hill. There below us was the town and the sea. It seemed like another world up there: fresh air, sunshine, and the faint noise of singing from the Cathedral mingling with the distant hum of the town.

We went into the Church to find a Roman Catholic Mass in progress. The priests and nuns were dressed in white and the whole scene had a wonderful freshness about it, a very strange sensation after the whirl and madness of everyday life. I must say that it was an experience I wouldn't have missed for the world.

All my love Mummsie, keep on writing and don't worry about me. I am having the time of my life at the moment. Love to all.
Tim

We had been taken up to Notre Dame d'Afrique by a Rifle Brigade captain, Robert Fellowes, about ten years older than us and who had lost a leg at Alamein and was now doing a base job. With Robert it was instant friendship. Tim in fact had been with him on the boat from England. Although we were only with him for such a short while, we both kept up a regular gossipy correspondence afterwards as if we had known him for years. It was he who introduced us to some members of a film company in what was officially known as the Transit Mess, but which I remember as merely an open courtyard with soft orange lights and crammed with black American merchant seamen in 'zoot suits', rather alarming. From there the film company people took us, minus the zoot suiters, to the office of the *Echo d'Alger* newspaper, where you pressed a secret bell and were let into a bar, and where no outsiders were supposed to be admitted – hence the notice *'Priez de ne pas parler haut et surtout de ne pas chanter.'* We all got exceedingly drunk on 'le zig-zag', made with anisette, so it was a case of the Wagons-Lits that night. I see that I described it as the 'maddest, wildest party I've ever been to'.

Letters had been arriving from friends at the front in Italy. I heard from Nick, who obviously was needing to unload some of his experiences – snow-drifts, a blizzard, nearly captured; but not half of the horrific story that I have since read in his *Beyond the Pale*. Bunny Roger was in hospital*; we gathered someone who had been at York with us was said to have been blinded.

These stories oddly made us all the more anxious to get out to Italy. They certainly must have contributed to our frenetic behaviour. I think they also heightened our appreciation of the beautiful country around us. I noticed that after getting those letters Tim would sometimes say a prayer before getting into bed. It was a little embarrassing. I felt I should have done the same . . .

We applied to join the Parachute Regiment but were turned down.

2nd February, 1944

Many very happy returns of 4th February. I shall think of you. I sent a Moroccan leather thing to keep letters in. I hope it arrives safely.

I still am having a wickedly good time; it doesn't seem right that one should go abroad to fight and then have a glorious time, but all the same I shall enjoy all I possibly can until something happens.

Today is the nearest thing to heaven imaginable – boiling, baking sun, and nothing to do but enjoy it. I am spending it swimming and sunbathing in a little cove we have discovered, not unlike 'our' cove at Portmeirion, except that it is almost a

---

*Bunny has reassured me that he was only in hospital for one night with water on the knee.

lagoon surrounded by great red rocks forming a sort of frame for the view of Algiers; white against the green hillside across the blue bay. Great waves crash through the opening, leaving about 20 yards of yellow sand for us to bathe on. No one else seems to have found it yet, so we newcomers can sun our somewhat white bodies without being stared at. [We called it the Sea-Witch Cauldron.]

The other day we went up into the mountains. Oh, how I wish you could have been there. As we climbed up, we passed through almost Italian country – red-roofed houses surrounded with almond trees in full blossom. Then came Switzerland in summer, Arab children standing on the roadside offering us bunches of gentians and wild iris. I thought of the time that we picked those gentians up on Monte Mottarone. Finally we arrived at the top. Switzerland in winter, what a contrast; snow on the ground, and that particular intoxicating smell of pines in the frosty air. We went to the restaurant and drank large thick cups of café-au-lait, so like the first time we went to Switzerland. Do you remember the first morning on the railway station? And the coffee there?

My love to everyone, and most of all to you. Tim

In my diary I had written about my 'moods'. One night, very soon after that trip, which had been with Robert Fellowes, up to the mountain village (called Chreá), I had a really black one. At the *Echo d'Alger* bar there was the usual collection of much older American army people, male and female, plus exotic characters such as Madame Matthieu the tennis player and Josephine Baker's dancing partner. I suddenly felt that I had had enough. I was wasting my time, fed up with the sexual undertones; and anyway who cared whether I was there or not? I didn't know much about tennis, had never been to Wimbledon. So I left without telling Tim or anybody else. It was a severe case of what we called Algeriana. Suddenly I was hating Algiers. It was sordid, cruel, heartless. I took a taxi to the Wagons-Lits. Somewhere, out there among the cranes and funnels of the docks, I heard a long drawn-out cry like someone being knifed. At that moment, my lowest ebb, an Army truck appeared. It was going to La Pérouse, and I thankfully accepted a lift.

Tim arrived the next morning, and I broke down. We had a long talk, and I ended feeling a fool. We then heard that in about ten days we were to be sent to Italy, and that therefore we could have some special leave. We decided to spend it on a tour organized by the Thomas Cook office to the oasis of Bou-Saada, on the other side of the Little Atlas. It was the perfect antidote to my depression, which was thereupon forgotten. In his next letters to his mother Tim did not mention that we were about to go abroad.

10th February, 1944

I am writing this letter from the Oasis of Bou-Saada on the edge of the Sahara desert, where I am spending four days' leave. Leave doesn't seem right without you and Pipewell, but this is the next best thing possible.

We left Algiers by bus, and what a bus – rather like a hat box on wheels, with an engine I am certain was run on brandy! All sorts of explosions before the thing would go at all. Not surprising as the vehicle was twice as full as it should have been, and had baggage piled high on top. All the fellow passengers were Arabs who had brought everything with them including hens, which clucked and made messes all the time. The journey was lovely – through the Atlas mountains and over the desert. This place is past belief. One is quite dazed, and can't cope at all. Tomorrow I will write more. The thing that has struck me most is that this hotel has a real WC, also a plug and beaucoup de papier! Such luxury.

11th February, evening. We had a grand day – breakfast on the balcony with croissants and honey. At 10 a.m. we went out into the desert on camels. I thought of you riding a camel at Cairo. I can't think how you did it, because I was nearly sea-sick. We came back to the town in time to go round the wonderful mudhoused streets before lunch. It was too like a film for words – brilliant colours and wonderful jewels – one expected to see Marlene Dietrich coming out of the Garden of Allah at any moment. We went inside an Arab house and saw the woman making bread, an extraordinary process: mixing and beating on the floor, and finally throwing it into the fire, where it sizzled until it was nearly burning. Then without any more ceremony they wolfed it in one mouthful. This afternoon we hired Arab steeds and rode across the desert to some ravines among the rocks. It was heaven. Galloping, galloping, galloping across the wide open spaces. I thought I had forgotten how to sit on a horse, but it all came back quite quickly. The guide was a wonderful individual. Tall and dusky with a fez and milk white cloak embroidered in red. He led the way at high speed on his black pony. All the horses here are quite beautiful, sleek and wiry. I had a white one which went like the wind . . .

All my love – I think of you all the time, Tim

13th February, 1944

I hope you will get my letter from Bou-Saada at the same time as this, then you will treat most of it as a continuation. I must say the last few days have been more unreal than anything else so far. The glorious peace of being away from the army for a bit, and the strangeness of being out in the desert and away from Europeans – it was another world.

We had a good journey back – with lots of hens in the bus, and across the mountains. I hoped to get some letters when I got back, but there were none. . . . I do love North Africa, it seems to grow on one. I hated the Arabs at first, but now I have grown very fond of them. The piccaninnies are sweet, and I have two particular ones called Ali and Mohammet, aged four, who follow me around the village and eat my chewing gum ration. The other day they came rushing up when I was doing a route march and presented me with an egg! I shall miss them very much when I leave.

The weather this last few days has been quite appalling, rain and very cold wind. It just doesn't make sense after the lovely weather we have been having. . . . You may not hear from me for some time now – but please write and write and write to the address at the top of this letter.

All my love my darling Mummie, Tim

On the 16th I wrote: 'Casualties in Italy frightful. Just heard so many people I know missing.' The rain had turned to snow. Snow in Algiers, it seemed impossible. In two days' time our draft would be off. Now I felt I was going to miss our 'Wogs'. 'But perhaps it's just as well. Things are getting pretty stale.' In his inimitable way Tim set about cheering us all up. Other Rifle

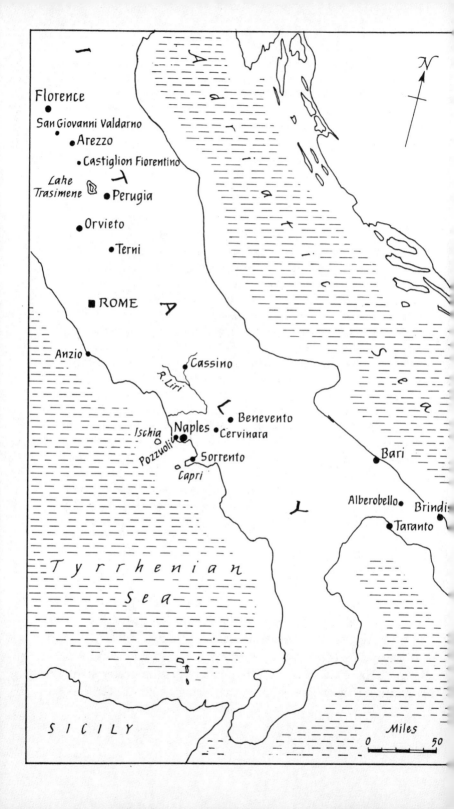

N

Florence
San Giovanni Valdarno
Arezzo
Castiglion Fiorentino
Lake Trasimene
Perugia
Orvieto
Terni
ROME
Anzio
Cassino
R. Liri
Benevento
Ischia
Naples
Cervinara
Pozzuoli
Sorrento
Capri
Bari
Alberobello
Brindisi
Taranto

T y r r h e n i a n

S e a

S I C I L Y

Miles
0   50

Brigade officers were invited to the Juke Box. A new cocktail was invented, mostly *mousseux gazéifié*, with a dash of the usual cognac, and he did an imitation of the Ouëd Naïl belly dancing we had seen at Bou-Saada. We talked of the Italian Lakes and Venice. But we were going to Naples, the O *sole mio* Naples. Capri. Vesuvius. *The Story of San Michele*. The novels of Francis Brett Young. Nelson and Lady Hamilton. Romance!

23rd February, 1944

Here I am in Italy. Alas, it is not the Italy we knew in 1938. Today it is a sad and desolate country – no gay colour-washed houses. No fat smiling women sitting in the doorways with bambinos on their knees. They are white and sullen these days, and pad about the streets begging for food. I only saw Naples for a short time, but that was long enough to see the conditions. The streets seemed to be full of funeral processions (I suppose typhus victims) and starving people. They just crouch among their ruined houses or grovel in the dustbins looking for food. We can never be thankful enough that England wasn't invaded after Dunkirk. To think that all this might have happened to *our* people is too dreadful to contemplate.

The winter is still here. After North Africa it seems very cold and bleak – but the fine weather should come soon, and maybe, with it, some sort of relief for the Italians. I do so hope some of Italy will be spared this hell. It is such a lovely country, and it makes one feel so depressed to see all the glorious buildings shattered and just heaps of rubble, but I know it must be that way now, and thank God I have become quite numb to it all.

I don't think there is very much chance of me getting to a Rifle Bde battalion now. It would mean waiting, and I think one's personal feelings over regiments etc., should go, as after all the only thing that really matters is getting this war finished as soon as possible, and if one is of more use elsewhere, one should not object.

I got some letters when I arrived here, but unfortunately none from you or home as they were forwarded to North Africa before I arrived. But just keep on writing and eventually I will get some.

I saw some primroses in a wood today, very like the wood at Pipewell at this time of year. There is an old chapel in the middle with a saint's skull in a glass case – like the one at Santa Caterina, do you remember? It is all rather like *Grimms' Fairy Tales*; little castles perched on the hillside and horses with silver harnesses.

Mummsie, I can't tell you how pleased I am that I have been out here and seen first hand all the things I have mentioned in this letter, and all the other things I have written about in the past. It does make one realize deeply how lucky we are in England, and what a wonderful country it is. After this war we must all see that peace is sensibly planned so that all this can never happen again.

All my love Mummsie darling, I must stop because I have run out of candles and this one is just about finished. I think of you so much. Look after yourself, Tim

We were at Paolisi, a village between Naples and Benevento. Our arrival at Naples had been the 'full' disappointment. For one thing there was still snow. Vesuvius was under clouds. Docks a shambles. Husks of buildings. Everywhere you saw beggars, and there were notices about the dangers of VD in the area, and how lice caused typhus. We were driven off in a three-tonner to Paolisi. Here too were misery and ugliness, people starving. No snow but driving rain and mud. There were more rumours of friends dead and wounded, or taken prisoner. 'Our clothes are damp,' I wrote in my diary, 'and there are pools in our tents. We shiver round oil stoves in the gaunt stone building that is our mess. Cooking is a nightmare, and the food is the eternal bully or M & V [tinned meat and vegetables]. But we cannot complain. To think of Nick and Henry up there in their slit-trenches, with only one blanket. At night you see the flashes of artillery from the front over bare sugar-loaf hills. Trucks rumble northwards all day through narrow cobbled streets. One tries so hard not to be a coward. But to see the misery and *appalling* poverty, the shattered buildings, grown men scrabbling for a crust, children in rags begging: it tears the heart from the roots. Last night in the darkness we met a little child of about three stumbling from the cookhouse where he had been to beg. He was moaning to himself and dead cold. That symbolizes war to me. . . .'

The weather suddenly lifted. We had been delighted to find Jimmy Stevens at Paolisi. He was such a good, solid, reliable person, never saying anything against anybody. The three of us climbed into the woods, finding wild narcissi, and came across the chapel that Tim described in his letter. And, yes, there were castles on the hilltops. We were joined by some children who gave us primroses. They called Tim Toumi and from then onwards he was known as that to Jimmy and me.

We hitched into Naples and saw Pompeii, eating our sandwiches in the Forum. Tim made us pretend we were ancient Romans. His sandals pinched terribly, he told us. We must call on that old bag Letitia and admire her frescoes. All those carts rumbling past. . . . The traffic was terrible these days . . .

We saw *Madam Butterfly* at the San Carlo, and laughed at stage-hands in the background waving large green fans studded with lights to imitate fire-flies. The officers' mess was in part of the Royal Palace, and there a crazy old peroxided tart sang *Ciri-Biri-Bin* and *Funiculi, funicula*.

Then at last Tim and I, not Jimmy, but with others such as John Macalpine, were told that we were to be transferred to the Green Howards.

This next letter was written by Tim to his brother David. The explanation given is that David was the sort of person who liked to shock, and had a 'lavatorial' sense of humour.

(undated)

Dear Brother,

I thought that as M.13 Sanitary of BNAF and CMF it was my duty to send a full report on conditions out here to you and your drainage company.

Let me start with North Africa (BNAF). I found the Arabs very careless in their habits. Street corners seemed to be favoured for after breakfast activities, and paper was unheard of. That is why the left hand is known as 'the unclean hand' in Mohammedan circles. Modern conveniences such as urinals are sadly abused. It is a common sight in Algiers to see Arab gentlemen squatting firmly in them with their backs to the wall making the oddest noises. In the more exclusive houses a hole about one foot in diameter is provided at the top of the house for the convenience of the family, over which one can stand or squat as the case may be. Why it should be at the top I don't know, except that it makes a satisfactory noise when it hits the street below. We in the better regiments of the British Army favour the 'Thunder Box' as our sanitary furniture. Quite easily made by cutting a hole in the top of a tea chest and placing it over a pit in the ground about six feet in depth. The name describes it completely as the sound-transmitting powers of a tea chest are TREMENDOUS! A 'four gallon petrol tin' is a nice alternative to the above method, not so comfortable but adequate, and care must be taken when rising otherwise grave wounds will be suffered through jagged edges.

On the Italian front conditions are very much the same, except for one addition that I feel I should mention. That is 'the flowered bowl' which I came across in the palace of a very wealthy duchessa. At first it appeared to be an ordinary water closet without a plug, but when I looked closer I found that the pan itself was a very smart bowl decorated with pink roses, but with no hole in it. On further inspection I found a lever at the side which I lifted. This caused the bowl to be turned upside down and whatever might be inside it to be thrown into the chasm below. EXTREME caution must be exercised when using this piece of furniture, and it is *essential* to rise slightly from the seat before flushing as any part of the body below the level of the seat will receive a nasty blow from the revolving bowl. I learnt this fact from my own discomfort.

Well, brother, my first despatch must come to a close. I feel sure it will be of valuable assistance to you and your company in the future.

I remain, Sir, your obedient Sanitary Officer, Lt Sir Timothy Tightarse Bart (Please note, these facts are not for publication, without permission of the War Office, Ministry of Drains and the Savoy.)

To his mother Tim wrote:

1st March, 1944

Here I am at last with a unit; not the Rifle Bde, but the next best thing, as there are a lot of Rifle Bde officers in it. I am settling down well now, but it was strange at first. I knew nothing about the regiment, but as it turns out they are first class people [many being Yorkshire miners].

I went to Pompeii last Sunday for the day. I had no idea it was so well preserved; some of the designs on the walls of the houses are quite perfect in form and colour. I always thought that Roman decoration would be crude and rather slap-dash, but it is in fact just the opposite. The frescoes are done in the smallest detail, and beautifully finished. The thing that impressed me most, I think, was the gay colouring of the floors, which blended exactly with the rest of the décor. I wish I had had more time to study and take down some of the designs. By the way, I got a little statuette for you which I thought was rather nice, and it is on its way home now. I do hope you like it.

I had a lovely journey up through the mountains coming here. It was raining hard unfortunately, but the little villages still looked very attractive, climbing up the hillsides. This country reminds me so much of Wales and consequently of you; not so much of home and the north of England. The campaniles are all like the one at Portmeirion, and have the same spiked tops and at the moment the mountains have that Welsh greyness.

You would laugh if you could see me now, sitting in bed in a large room with a domed ceiling, feeling like a duke at least. But the only thing is that the Italians who live here have to come through to get to their rooms, so the traffic is not unlike Kettering on market day. Whenever I am getting dressed there seems to be a rush on, and they swarm through, saying 'Buon Giorno' to me with no trousers on – nature in the raw.

Don't worry about me, I am quite happy. I am sorry about the Rifle Bde, but fate seems to have taken a hand so often in my life and it has never let me down yet, so maybe it is all for the best . . .

I somehow feel very much in touch with you, even though I have no letters. Give my love to everyone, and God keep you safe for me. Tim

Now we were at Minturno, very close to the front at Cassino and billeted in private houses. My memories of Minturno are all in sepia. The sky was sepia, the mud was sepia, the face of our hostess, a frightened middle-class woman, was sepia. The guns were roaring. The buildings shuddered. Not a hint of all this in Tim's letter.

In the mess at lunchtime we were suddenly told that we were going back to Naples, en route for Anzio with the Green Howards, that very evening. Obviously there was some sort of panic up there.

Tim came up looking white. 'I've got some sores,' he said. 'The MO says I mustn't go with the battalion to Anzio.' Much later he wrote to me to say he had scabies.

I have been in hospital for the last few days with some beastly skin disease caused by the mud. Having been thoroughly de-loused I hope to be out again tomorrow or the next day.

Nothing very much to report from here, except that this place [Naples] has a lovely view across what is meant to be the most beautiful bay in the world. Owing to the weather I am not certain that I agree! Give me North Africa every time for weather, beauty and above all people. The Arabs may be dirty and crooked but they have personality at least. The Italians really are the end, to put it mildly. Just as dirty as Arabs (in their habits), and have a complete lack of principles. The fate of their country seems to mean nothing to them. The rich class are the ones I am referring to now. They sit about in the cafés talking and joking, while the working classes starve and beg for food. If you have the money in this country anything can be bought, at a price. Chocolate cakes and buns at 2/6d each. Glorious jewels and silks at huge prices. But the amazing thing is they are bought. Yesterday I saw an oily man of about 28 sitting and having tea with a girl covered in fur and jewels. Their bill for tea was about £2, just an ordinary tea with patisserie. He paid the bill as if it were 2/– and walked off. While round the corner a woman with five children was grovelling in the gutter picking up nuts which had been dropped by a fruit vendor. Fascism seems to have been blown out like a candle. Six months ago I suppose all these young men were ardent Fascists. Today they are quite willing to sit back and be happy under our rule.

It is so difficult to realize that these are the people who own this lovely country, and the people who were such wonderful artists and designers. It is rather interesting to note that the mosaic pottery and furniture designs here are dreadful, cheap and copies of the American modern stuff. They seem to have lost their creative gifts completely.

Please go on writing to me at the 1st Bn Green Howards, as I hope to be back soon. All my love to you and all, Tim

9th March (I think)

Here I am out of hospital, but not yet back with my unit.

I thought I must write and tell you that at last I have found a little town that is still what I call 'Italian'. Thank God it seems to have been spared the horror of war completely. I can't tell you its name, but at least I can describe it.

14. "The FANY was called Diana ('Dipsy') Portman" (p.29).

15. Raleigh Trevelyan in Rome, November, 1944.

16. "In her museum at Cavendish in Suffolk she [Sue Ryder] has on display her Sam Browne belt signed by Peter Ustinov, Eddie McGrigor and Tim" (p.29).

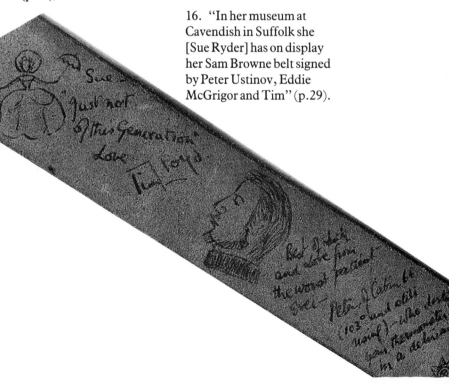

17. Tim in Naples wearing his fashionable Savile Row overcoat, March, 1944.

18. Charles Newton, 21 May, 1944, at Anzio, with Sergeant Edmonds, briefing his very young platoon before the breakout from the Beachhead. Many were killed or wounded two days later, and it was suggested that Charles should be recommended for a posthumous V.C.

19. Mornington Sutton, a private in Raleigh Trevelyan's platoon, is carried by two captured German soldiers after stepping on a mine during the breakout from the Anzio Beachhead, 23 May, 1944.

my little "TROLLI". I live in the voom on the vight – and breakfast on the varranda in the front –

20. "A village of funny little houses called 'Trulli'" (p.71).

21. 'On the road to Florence'.

22. Tim and Jimmy Stevens riding on bullocks (p.89).

23. Tim with Jimmy Stevens.

24. 'A camp among the olive trees in Tuscany'. These drawings are taken from Edward Seago's *With the Allied Armies in Italy*, given to Raleigh Trevelyan by the Collins family in 1945.

25. 'On the banks of the River Rubicon.'

There are no main roads leading to this town, it has sprung up right in the middle of a large plain. One minute you are on a cart track leading through the vineyards, and the next you are in the cobbled streets. Colour-washed buildings and palm trees around the market square. On one side there is a church with campanile crowned with a green 'onion'. On the other side there is the 'Palazzo Municipale' with broad shallow steps leading up to the wrought iron gates. A wonderful peace presides over the whole place – no noisy trucks and tanks.

Ferro Antonia

Ferro Alfonso

16th March I am not going back to the Green Howards. I must explain the strange writing above, they are the signatures of two sweet little children I met the other day. I was sitting up in the wayside eating sandwiches and I heard singing in the distance. I looked up and saw a small boy and girl coming down the hillside with a goat. When they saw me they came up and sat down beside me on the bank. After a few minutes of rapid Italian on my part, they were quite happy in sharing my sandwiches with me. After lunch they sang in harmony with the most lovely little voices, so simple and unselfconscious. After about half an hour they jumped up and raced away down the hillside, with the goat leaping behind them. Tim

The little town would have been Rotondi, not far from Paolisi. Meanwhile I had begun my long stint in the trenches of Anzio. It was some months before I saw Tim again.

57

Life is fairly quiet here; I hope to go to the Rifle Bde soon. I don't pin my hopes on it because so many things have gone wrong in the past.

I haven't heard from you for ages, but I am not in the least worried because I know you are alright. It is very strange, but I feel so near to you at night when I say my prayers. I can just imagine you in the evening sitting in front of the fire in your room with all your favourite things around you. I am so pleased I saw your sitting-room before I went abroad. It is so lovely.

I do hope you understand this next bit.

One thing at least I have learned out here, and that is to trust God completely. Whatever happens, there is always a meaning to it, and it is for the best in the end. You have always taught me that, and you showed me the meaning of it when Daddy died. I shall never forget the wonderful calm way that you walked into church on the day of the funeral, your head erect and trusting God to bring you through that ordeal. He did bring you through, and all the time at Portmeirion I felt that some great power was helping and comforting you in a way that no human being could possibly have done. We are so small, and without that faith life is too bewildering and hard; but with it one can overcome *any* obstacle.

When I went up to the line first I felt I wasn't ready. My mind was muddled, and everything seemed too dreadful for words. Death, misery, unhappiness all seemed unbelievably terrible. Then I got that skin disease, and I have had time to get my mind adapted and sort out various things. Now I feel happy and confident. With God's help I can and will overcome all the things that have worried me. He will give me strength and help me. It is so difficult to put down one's feelings on paper, but I do hope you understand what I have tried to say.

I had a letter from Michael King the other day, saying that Pen had thought he was me! He was the very best friend at Ranby and we shared a room together. Everyone said that we were so alike. I do wish he could have come out with me.

I am glad that I am no longer with the Green Howards. But here it is so important that one should be with people one can get on with easily, and somehow they were very queer types. It isn't just snobbishness I can assure you – just that they cannot understand public school people, and are jealous because one has been brought up in what they call 'a posh house'. I met an officer in the Recce Corps called Freddie Marsh whose father is a farmer near Rushton. He was quite pleasant, but rather difficult to get on with because, I think, he felt the difference of status rather.

Don't worry, Mummsie. It will all work out. If I don't join the RBs, I shall transfer to the Guards. I mentioned it to them the other day, and they said it would be quite possible, and would like to have me. I have met so many Guardees, all very much like me and with so many with kindred interests. All my love. I think of you so much. No letters from you are dull, so don't say they are. Tim

19th March, 1944

The most lovely day. I am sitting on the hillside looking over a little village which tumbles down to the plain below. It looks like a toy village from here. Red roofs clustered round the campanile and church which forms the nucleus for the narrow streets and twisted stairways. Distant sounds of cartwheels and hammering drift up from below, and there are sounds of singing from the foresters and children in the woods. Above it all a church bell comes ringing clear across the valley, echoing against the snow-capped crags opposite. Spring must be nearly here. I can tell that by the snowdrops which push their way through last year's chestnut leaves. Everything is gay and fresh today; even the women sing and smile as they bounce down the hillside with heavy faggots balanced on their heads. Clip-clop go their wooden shoes against the rocks.

Nature's miracle has started once more. Oh how wonderful it is to be alive.

All my love, Tim

22nd March, 1944

Today is my birthday, this time a day which has been marked by an almost unique experience. The great mountain Vesuvius has once again erupted. I took a truck this morning and went to see what I could of it. It really was amazing, a huge river of bubbling lava oozing down the mountainside, in places I am told ninety foot deep and a quarter of a mile wide. I was able to get about a mile and a half from the rolling torrent, which was making a sort of hissing noise – even at that distance the heat was terrific. The top of the mountain was blood red,

The above must NOT be completed.

21 MAR 1944

TO:- Mʳˢ S J. LLOYD
PIPEWELL HALL
KETTERING.
ENGLAND   NORTHANTS

843164

Write the message very plainly below this line.

Sender's Address

PEASANTS.
GOING TO WORK. ITALY 44.

This space should not be used.

with an occasional flame of yellow as it belched out rocks and burning clinker. Smoke and steam hung over two towns which are in grave danger of being covered. Civilians were fleeing along the narrow roads carrying bedding on their heads and all their worldly goods slung around them. The peasants were almost hysterical over the whole incident, as many legends and superstitions have grown up about an eruption that will bring the end of the world.

The Americans have come to the fore bringing army trucks etc., to evacuate the towns and homesteads in danger. Maybe I was only just in time when I went to Pompeii the other day . . .

Mummie darling, I understand very well the way you feel now about the Spring and your walks being pointless because Daddy isn't here to enjoy them with you. I sometimes feel the same, but in a smaller way – a lot of my dearest friends have been killed lately, and life somehow loses so much of its kick and joy. But there are so many other people who go on giving happiness, life will never be pointless. I think the same thing applies to you. The whole family depends on you, and I can't tell you how much your love and thoughts mean to me. I think so much of you, and long to be back home with you. I know that this can't be – yet – but some day I will be back, and all the wonderful sights and experiences which I have shared in my mind with you will make our reunion much greater. In the same way I feel that when you meet Daddy in the afterlife, all the Springs and beautiful things you have shared with him in your mind will not be lost.

I had an excellent letter from Pierre yesterday, telling me about Deborah's cocktail party. Too funny about the Americans wanting her address and telephone number! I would love to have been able to take her to her first Queen Charlotte's ball.

All my love, Tim

26 *March*, 1944

I must write to tell you that the Guards accepted me for transfer a few days ago. I was to have joined the Coldstream, but the Rifle Brigade will not release me. So *now* I think they are almost certain to send me to a Battalion, but one can never tell. They have made a mess of things so many times before.

I went to Naples yesterday and met lots of old friends, two of whom you know. . . . We had a riotous dinner party last night at a restaurant called the Orange Grove overlooking the Bay. I adore Naples now. The sunshine makes all the difference. I think

I have been lucky as Vesuvius is looking quite fantastic at the moment. I watched the sunset last night and I'll try to jot down a description . . .

Vesuvius still belching thick grey smoke into the clear blue sky. Up and up it twirls like a giant column of cotton wool, 20,000 feet above the crater. The huge mountains tower above the white Naples, clinging to the edge of the Bay. . . . Another eruption . . . bruuuuumph! Down the side rushes the fiery lava, followed by a cloud of smoke and steam. The sun is red, the sky is red. It seems that the whole world is on fire. The only other colour is the still blue of the Bay in which the whole picture is reflected. How small I feel sitting here, watching the strength and fury of this great mountain. Already she has destroyed two complete towns, and others are in danger. No wonder the peasants think that the End of the World has come. No sooner has the war passed them by than the earth declares war and destroys their homes and vineyards.

I had a letter from Raleigh Trevelyan today (the man who shared my room in Africa). He is at Anzio and having a beastly time, living in a trench knee-deep in mud and only eighty yards from the Germans. Not a very pleasant situation, to say the least of it. I think my skin disease must have been a blessing in disguise.

I am sorry to say that Freddie Marsh (the boy who lives near Rushton) is missing believed killed. He was very nice when you got past the mask of the Army. Please don't mention this to anyone out of the family, as his parents may not know yet, and it is possible that he will turn up.

So wonderful, I received a package of re-directed mail today, 25 letters, 10 of which were from you, some written as far back as November. Now I can fill in the gaps . . .

Every night I sleep in the sleeping bag you gave me and I bless you for it. All my love, Tim

8th April, 1944

How sweet the Italian children are. Lately I have been taking my lunch (spam, bread and wine) onto the mountainside. One day two little children came and shared it with me. They are so like wild creatures, long unruly hair, bare feet, and clad in rags of various bright colours, leaping and dancing among the fresh new grass and wild flowers. Timid at first when I offered them food, but soon laughing and happy when they saw I meant no harm. The next day there were five waiting for me, and today as I walked through the village no less than ten followed me up the hillside. I felt rather like the Pied Piper of Hamelin! After lunch they all rushed off and came back with bunches of primroses to give me for the Madonna's festa, and explained that I must go with them tomorrow up the mountain to the monastery where there is a mass for the Madonna on Easter Day. There is something so charmingly simple about these children. They live a life of poverty, but are still happy, singing and playing all day long with the birds and beasts.

Easter Sunday
Such a lovely day. I got up at 6 a.m. to go up to the monastery, and met the children in the street. Off we went, up the mountainside and through the woods to the monastery, which stands on a spur two thousand feet up above the valley. All the way up little parties joined us, until there was a stream of peasants climbing up and up. By half past seven we were standing under the arches watching the sun shining down on the valley below. Everything was still except for the sounds of voices and the bells drifting up from below. The cracked bell in the campanile above me had stopped its call, and the priest was preparing the mass. There were too many people to get inside the church, so they overflowed onto the hillside behind, where they sat in silence while the service went on – singing the chants and joining in as best they could. After the service my young companions dragged me away to a glade a hundred yards away where tables had been erected for the festa meal. Down we sat, and ate cakes and drank wine. The band struck up and the dancing began. All I could do was to sit and watch, spell-bound by the simple charm of these people. The children gave me nuts, nougat, bread, everything I could want and refused to take anything in return. At 11 a.m. the bell started ringing, and we all formed up into line to carry the Madonna to the village below. First in the procession came the Pastor in a surplice made of priceless lace. Then the Madonna sitting on a golden throne, carried on the shoulders of the young men of the village. Following them were the girls who sang songs all the way down. The band came next and then all the rest of the people bare-headed and walking in couples. I ran on ahead to watch the procession winding down the narrow track, the pure

voices of the women echoing across the mountains, the bells ringing in the village below to welcome the Blessed Madonna. What natural blending of colour – the pink monastery, the green grass, and oh so many bright blues and reds, and every colour under the rainbow in the cloaks of the worshippers. When we got down to the village the streets were thick with people and the balconies crowded with children throwing bunches of primroses and camellias on to the procession below. The ground was covered with blossom petals and wild flowers, and as we reached the village church women ran forward with gifts of money for the Madonna. How far away from the war it all seemed. 'Peace on Earth and Goodwill to all men' was the order of the day, but to the army and me just another of those incidents that fills our rather dreamlike lives.

I enclose a picture of the Madonna della Stella which was given to me by one of the children. Will you keep it for me? All my love, Tim

Easter Day, 1944

I thought of you so much today, and longed for you to be with me. I enclose a quick sketch of the 'Festa della Madonna' and a few olive leaves from the monastery. Also a little cross. The photo is just a press cutting of a village just like this one – arches and stairways galore. How I wish the vehicle was a farm cart and not a Bren gun carrier. All my love, darling Mummie, Timmy

11th April, 1944

The Spring is really here now. After the damp and cold of living under canvas, the fine weather is unbelievably welcome! All the blossom is out and everywhere is covered with that lovely fresh green. This once dreary valley is transformed into a paradise of colour and happiness. Nature works on me like a tonic, even though I haven't been well. . . . The nervous strain has been rather heavy.

I am sitting now in a little sunken garden behind the mess under a fruit tree heavy with blossom. If I look up I can see tracery of the branches against the clear blue sky. How soft and fluffy the blossom looks, and how beautifully it fits in with the hard lines of the branches. Occasionally petals flutter down and settle on the grass around me. Against the wall on my right is a camellia tree dripping with blood red buds; some of the flowers are out at the top where they catch the sun, large and waxy like the artificial ones at Fortnums. Looking at the hillside I

EASTER DAY 1944.
    The procession of the Madonna Della Stella — coming down the Mountain
    side — from the Monastery to Rotundi.

65

can see the shepherd bringing his sheep down to the village. Tinkle ... clank, tinkle ... clank, the bells go, as they make their way down the narrow path. It's getting dark so I must go into dinner. Good night Mummsie.

April 12th

Another glorious day, but unfortunately somewhat marred by my having to go to hospital, this time with impetigo. I have had it for the last few days, and now it has spread to my hair which will have to be shaved off! Isn't it sickening? I seem to be like a rotten apple these days, always coming up in bumps and going bad. I think it must be living in dirt the whole time and never being able to have a proper bath.

Later. 10 p.m.

You should see me now. As Roo would say, 'You would die of laughing': head done up in a turban and a white plaster mask on my face; looking not unlike an Elizabeth Arden advertisement! What one goes through for beauty. They haven't taken all my hair off yet, just the back and sides, leaving me a fuzzy bit in front!! I do hope I won't have to be here long, as it is so lovely outside. All the same it is a luxury to sleep on a bed and one with sheets. This hospital, in better times, was a palace belonging to a very famous duke [presumably Aosta]. From the window I can see the gardens stretching away for three miles, believe it or not – going in terraces up the hillside with fountains etc. I can't wait to get out and look more closely.

Do you realize that just five years ago this week we were together at Cadenabbia? It doesn't seem as long as that does it? I still remember every little detail; spaghetti under the plane trees – the rhodies in the Villa Carlotta's garden, our £5 trip to St Moritz, and of course you begging £1 off the Cook's man at Lugano! We will go there again one day, Mummie, and they won't cheat us at the hotel desk next time.

My love to Everybody, and tons and tons to you, Timmy

Since I wrote to you last I have been evacuated to another hospital further south. I arrived at this lovely place yesterday after a journey across Italy by ambulance train. Quite a good journey except that we passed over the mountains at night which was a bore, but had the advantage of seeing the Adriatic for the first time at sunrise. I hope to see the mountains on the way back. I can't tell you where I am except that it is somewhere in the heel of Italy [it was near Brindisi] and on the coast, so just take out a map and have a look.

I had a peep at the town on the way up in the ambulance from the station. It struck me as usual as being quite unreal. Pink and white houses covered with wistaria and vines just sprouting leaves. Giant pointed cacti shooting from the top of garden walls – in fact musical comedy Italy in the flesh. It is all very lovely, but oh how I long for sanity and something real. Somehow since I left England, life has been one long whirl of dream like always in places like this.

Excuse the upside down writing, but that is how life strikes me at the present. A complete mixture of Heaven and Hell. One minute one is speechless because of the *wonderful* sights and sunshine, and the next one comes back to earth with a bump and one realizes why one is here at all. There is one thing that never changes, and that is the anchor that we both have and will always have. Without that I would be like a ship without a compass, but with the faith that is always with me I can enjoy the lovely things and put up with the others. Goodnight my darling Mummie; will write more tomorrow.

April 23rd

Shakespeare's birthday. I always think of Stratford at this time of the year and remember the wonderful times I had there. My impetigo is much better. Today I hitchhiked out to a little fishing village along the coast. I walked out along the mole of an ideal harbour, and looked at the little fishing boats with their rust-coloured sails and nets drying in the sun: a foreground for the pink and white houses of the village and the campanile pointing to the sky. There seems to be quite a Balkan influence here, as all the churches have domes and 'onion' tops to the campaniles. Also there are many more flat roofs this side of Italy. It is rather like North Africa – in fact just my cup of tea.

I can't make out the Italian attitude towards religion. I went into a church yesterday (Sunday) and found a lot of little urchins playing 'tig' round the pillars. By the font the priest was christening a child, quite unperturbed by the noise. As I walked round, looking at a rather lovely Madonna, a choir boy detached himself from the christening and came over to me. He looked at the statue and said 'Bella

Madonna', then in the next breath, 'Hey Tommy, give me chew gum!' And as I was leaving the church, one of the vergers rushed up and asked for cigarettes. I was somewhat shattered! . . .

I am going to see Marlene Dietrich today, who is here in Italy doing a troop show. I shall be able to see how like my puppet she was. All my love, Tim

He wrote to me about the Marlene Dietrich show. The letter was delivered when I was living under my cowshed, Smoky Joe's, and cheered me up a lot.

1st May, 1944

It is over a week since I wrote last, but somehow being in hospital there has been very little to write about. I had a relapse about a week ago, which was a bore as I thought I was getting on much better, so now I am back in bed. All the same life has been quite amusing, except that the M & B was rather sickmaking. Dipsy Portman and four other FANY girls have been in to see me at regular intervals, which is nice except that I don't look very beautiful with blue ointment all over my face and hair shorn at the back and sides! They were full of London gossip, and told me of so many of my friends who have got married lately. *Very* stupid I think at the moment, as who can tell how things will turn out in the next few months, and anyway it seems madness to take such final steps as that when everyone is emotional and unsettled about the future.

It must be lovely in England now, fresh green leaves and daffodils everywhere. May Day has so many memories for me; at Pipewell the children with their bunches of primroses, and at Stratford the May Day festivities. The sunshine here is wonderful, I do so long to get out and see the flowers and lilac which is in full bloom here. When I am better I am going to a convalescent home for a week or so. I believe it is quite fantastic – a villa up in the hills with a view of seven miles across the plain to the Adriatic. I can't imagine anything more fitting to my tastes. I will write to you all about it when I go there.

Oh Mummy, I have been so lucky out here. My life has been so easy compared with what other people have been through. I have been able to see so much more of the countries I have been in than most other people, and I thank God I have been able to appreciate them. I don't think I would have done nearly so much if I hadn't been abroad with you for the first time. You taught me how to enjoy lovely things to their best advantage. . . .

The Marlene Dietrich show was excellent. She is an amazing woman. She must be fifty if she is a day and still looks 25 even at close quarters. I being rather catty took a pair of field glasses, and even with them in the front row of the stalls not a *line* could I see! She is very clever too. She played the 'Barcarolle' with a violin bow on a carpenters' saw. I was surprised, as I thought all she could do was to look beautiful.

I have been reading about Saint Benedict. He was a remarkable man. I think it is dreadful to think that the Cassino monastery is no more, after the toil that was put into building it. When I saw it, it looked just like a mound of stones on the top of the hill. How I hate these Germans for all the hell they have brought to places of beauty and culture. Rome will be the next tragedy. What right have we as one stupid little generation to deprive all the men and women of the future of these wonderful things? 'C'est la guerre,' I suppose; the only answer one can give. Things that are made by man will always be destroyed by man. But one thing that can never be destroyed is natural beauty: the great mountains, seas, sunsets, the flowers and the trees; these things will always remain, and be a joy to people who can appreciate them.

Lots of love my darling Mummy. Give mine to everyone. Timmy

4th May, 1944

I am much better now and rather regret the depressing letter I sent a few days ago. I think it must have been the M & B that did it. My spots have gone like magic, and once again I can sit in the glorious sunshine. Somehow the sun is much more zip-making out here than in England. Even at night it is warm now. This evening I sat out on the hospital roof for half an hour after dinner, watching the lights of the town glittering like diamonds around me. It may not be a very inspiring view by day, but by night it is glorious. The moon is full tonight and the stars twinkle like mad. The world is quiet except for music coming from an open air cinema somewhere in the town. I think the film must be the 'Great Waltz', as bits of Strauss keep on filling the air. Too dreamy for words.

On Tuesday next I go to a convalescent home. It may be a monastery or the place I told you about in the last letter. Anyway both are in the country by the sea, so I don't mind. To bed now – goodnight.

8th May
Am out and about again now, and go to the 'Con. Home' tomorrow. I had lunch yesterday at the Officers' Hotel here, much the nicest one I have found yet. Very good and cheap Italian food. Upstairs there is a verandah with little round tables and huge gaudy umbrellas where one can sit and have tea overlooking the sea and fishing harbour. Luckily the wind always seems to blow in the right direction, so that one doesn't get the smell. Yesterday it was quite a peacetime scene. The men in white tropical clothes and a smattering of ENSA girls in gay dresses. It might almost have been the verandah at the Bellevue at Baveno. Oh how I wonder how the lakes look now. The azaleas will just be coming out in the Villa Carlotta's garden, and the rhodies will be in full bloom in the Villa Serbelloni at Bellagio. I suppose *our* hotel with those lovely rooms are full of fat German soldiers and their girlfriends on leave. It is all so near, but yet so far.

I do hope you will go to Portmeirion again this Spring. I want to be able to imagine you in the same sort of atmosphere that I am in. I suppose the hotel will be in full swing again now. I remember people were booking rooms for May when we were there in October, but you can always get in I am sure.

Lots of love. Look after yourself. I am always thinking of you, and longing for the day when I can see you again. Timmy

The convalescent home, run by the Red Cross, was at Alberobello, between Bari and Taranto, and famous for its *Trulli* houses, now a major tourist draw. He was lucky indeed to be there.

(undated)
I have been hoping all day to sit down and write about this wonderful home for lost souls. I arrived last evening to find an Italian paradise. Before the war it was a country colony for Fascist nobles. Perched high on the hillside looking over what I think must be one of the most beautiful valleys in Europe to

the Adriatic in the distance. It consists of a village of funny little houses called 'Trulli'. They look just like the houses in the old fairy tale books – with pointed conical roofs and twisted chimneys. I enclose a photo of the main street. The remainder of the village almost hangs over the edge of the Cliff.

The home is run exactly like a country club, with a restaurant and lots of little houses where you sleep and have breakfast. I have a room in an enchanting little gingerbread house with a verandah and garden – quite alone except for a sweet old Austrian couple who wait on me hand and foot. Their son was shot by the Germans for underground activities and the poor old man spent nine months in a concentration camp.

This morning I had breakfast in my dressing gown on the verandah: such LUXURY. The view is quite perfect – framed by the fig and almond trees in the garden below. After breakfast I put on my tropical trousers and went for a walk across the hill. I must say that it is quite the most quaint part of Italy I have seen yet. Little pink and white houses dotted among the olive trees and cornfields. The wild flowers are beyond belief. The ground is carpeted with poppies, cornflowers, magenta clover a foot tall, and quantities of wild michaelmas daisies.

The peasants carry pitchers of water to water the vines and huge bundles of green grass. I sat and listened to the cowbells ringing in the distance and I longed oh so much for you to be here. You would adore it, and cow bells will always remind me of you and Roo on Monte Mottarone at Stresa.

This afternoon we went by the Red Cross bus to swim. There is a lovely little bathing place in a cove among the rocks. The grass comes within ten yards of the sea here, and the wild iris grows almost on the water's edge. It was very hot and the water is crystal clear. At 4.30 p.m. sharp Italian waiters dressed in white coats appeared with tea and plates of goodies. It is so well organized that one can't believe that it is all free!

You have no idea how much we appreciate the small comforts out here, things like tea in the morning, sheets, BATHS, and above all an atmosphere that is so unarmyfied. The Red Cross certainly is a marvellous organization.

There was a dance last night, and Dipsy Portman turned up! I had no idea she was near here. We are going to Brindisi on Saturday to the Opera, which should be fun. The opera company is very good and is doing *Carmen*, so I am looking forward to it.

12 Midnight
After dinner tonight I met some very nice Italian people who took me and another boy to the local pub. How can one believe that there is a war so close when one looks at these peasants sitting round the tables smoking their clay pipes and red wine? Just a whitewashed room with a few old barrels in the corner, it must have been the same hundreds of years ago . . .

Love, Timmy

18th May, 1944
I am still having a wonderful time at this place, it is so uncivilized – by that I mean no cars, lorries etc. Yesterday I got a pony trap and took Sue Ryder (a friend of Mike King's in England) out for a drive in the country. We drove all over the place, to out of the way towns, villages, churches and a wonderful grotto. This countryside is very attractive with the quantities of Trulli houses dotted among the fig and olive groves. I find it hard to describe the beautiful Italian scenery. Ninety per cent of the time I think I am dreaming all this.

We drove back at twilight in the trap, which by this time had been decorated all over with flowers by the driver. Bunches of roses and gladioli on the shafts and a plume of wistaria on the horse's head.

These little Trulli houses are incredible, unique in fact. They are found only in this district and in Corsica. Built by the peasants, without any set plan. They start with one beehive, and as the  family grows they add as they think fit. I have seen some houses with as many as 15 little beehives. As the ground is very uneven you get some of the rooms leaning at an angle.

Babies are wrapped in bandages to a thickness of 3 inches and strapped in a pillow case for the first 6 months only allowed to be unwrapped twice daily (for obvious reasons). Mothers carry them on their backs when at work and bounce them on the floor for exercise. All my love, Tim

Sue Ryder writes of their expedition in *Child of My Love*: how they visited churches and heard Italians singing arias from Verdi. Looking back, she has remembered his faith and optimism, strangely mixed with a clear premonition. He had said to her, 'You will probably survive and go on and do things for the poor and the sick.' 'We listened to the birds, and talked about the value of faith.' The FANYs were living in remote secret places in the mountains and had to have special permission, which was rarely granted, to see people unconnected with their work.

20th May, 1944

I am still at the Red Cross home and am feeling in robust health now. Yesterday I gave an Italian lunch party at a little Trulli house right on the edge of the hillside. 3 FANY girls came, and a meal of spaghetti, risotto etc. was cooked by an old peasant signora. It really was very pleasant sitting on the crazy paved verandah and eating from a table loaded with good things. The peasants were thrilled, and we ate so much that we didn't finish lunch until 4.30, having started at 12.30. Their dress is very picturesque, and they always wear bright reds and blues over fantastic underclothes. The signora's dress kept on blowing up and revealed a pair of bloomers made of sea boot stocking wool!

There are quantities of cherries out now. You just pick them off the trees as you walk. I am getting quite bloated with all these good things. I shall have to start slimming down.

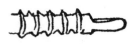 I have got a spaghetti rolling pin for you. It has grooves so that you can cut the pasta to the right size, as I have tried to show in the picture. I got it for three slices of bread! A good bargain don't you think?

You can get anything for white bread here, because the civilians get three slices of black bread a day and that is all, unless (which is always the case) they get more in the Black Market, and then it costs 400 Lire (£1 English money) a loaf! It is awful really because the Italians exist almost entirely on bread and spaghetti.

I shall be leaving here one day next week. Where I shall go I don't yet know. Anyway I have had a good rest, and will be quite ready to get back to work. The news seems better at the moment, and thank goodness Cassino has fallen. That has immense boosting value to us all, as it seemed that we would never be able to get on. I have had no news of any of my friends for ages now.

 I have sent you a little pitcher of wine like the one opposite. They are called a cucos in dialect and the peasants use them to take wine to the fields. I think they are rather fun and are a very good shape.

The wine is red vino that we all drink out here, as the water is bad. It is quite weak so please try to drink a little. The parcel should arrive in about a month or five weeks.

Please give my love to Roo and everyone, and tell them that I will answer letters as they arrive. All my love. I think of you so much – and long to get home to you. Timmy

One of the girls was Dipsy Portman. Another was Sue Ryder. In her letter to Tim's mother after his death Sue mentioned the cowbells and Tim buying the 'macaroni pin' and that 'queer earthenware bottle for vino' with a top made by a 'dear old peasant'.

Cassino having at last fallen, crucial battles were being fought on the roads to Rome. That day was all the more special because soon Tim would be leaving for the front. Sue had a presentiment that she would never see him again.

Just a note to let you know that I am out of the Red Cross Home and on my way north again. We stopped last night in this first class hotel at a seaside town [Bari]. I am now sitting in the sunshine at 7 a.m. waiting for coffee. Everything is very quiet, as it is still early. Only a few horse and carts clip clop along the waterfront. From where I am sitting the sea looks like a sheet of blue plate glass, absolutely calm except for ripples made by the red-sailed fishing boats. Across the harbour I can just see the majestic municipal buildings appearing through the heat haze. These were the pride of Mussolini's heart, as this place was to have become his 'back-door to the East'. It is a good thing Musso was stopped before he could spoil Italy altogether. His idea of beauty is not mine. He was pulling down all the old places and putting up creations looking like a mixture of Battersea Power Station and the Ritz Hotel.

Today is 1st June. I automatically think of last year. Strawberries and cream at Eton on 'the 4th', Deborah, Pierre, Billy and myself dining at the Berkeley. Then going to the Four Hundred with Charley Morpeth and the 'beautiful Prue'.

It seems rather a long way off from here. Sad in a way, but it will come again, and I am quite happy with the palm trees and sunshine in Italy. The weather is heavenly now. Yesterday we stopped for the afternoon on the seashore, as it was too hot for motoring in comfort. I swam in the green crystal-clear water and lay on the yellow sand with no clothes on. My North African suntan is back again now, and one can almost feel new life being soaked into one's bones as the sun beats down. After the war you and I are going to come and live for two months in a little Trulli house for £1 a week. I have got it all planned, even down to the old peasant woman who will 'do' for us. You will be able to write your memoirs, and I can paint and swim. I am learning Italian so that we will be able to get away from the beaten track and live with the Italians. I thought we might borrow an army truck and put all our belongings – beds, tins of tongue etc., and a portable 'Lav' (one must be practical) – in the back, then we would be self-supporting.

The news is wonderful at last. One can feel that the hell of last winter was worth it. Maybe soon I will be describing St Peter's in Rome to you.

All my love. Look after yourself. I will. Timmy

The Most Beautiful in The World

5th June, 1944

I am still on my way back north but have called for a night in Naples. You may remember that when I first came here I hated Naples, with its dirt and poverty, and felt I never wanted to see it again. But now summer is here, the sky is blue and the sea is even bluer, so at last I have seen the Bay as it should be seen and agree with the poets that perhaps this is the most majestic bay in the world.

At the moment I am lying on the rocks some five miles along the northern shore. Naples lies before me. From here it looks like a toy town with the pink and white buildings climbing up the dark green hill to the Castello which dominates the whole bay. Below it the dome of the Cathedral glints green in the sunshine, standing high above the house tops.

Vesuvius is behaving well again, quite quiet and only a small cloud round the summit. She wears this at a very jaunty angle like a woman wearing a new hat. Capri at the mouth of the bay is shrouded in a cloud of mist today, looking most mysterious and seductive. No wonder the mermaid legend comes from here. Anything might happen and one wouldn't think it odd. I can't claim to have seen a mermaid yet, but the Neapolitan girls who grace the rocks round here are the next best thing.

Later 8 p.m.

I am now dining at a little restaurant called Giuseppone a Mare, right on the seashore, with Naples glistening in the sun across the Bay. What more can I want, except to have you here with me. A little band of mandolins and guitars is playing all those lovely tenor songs that one used to hear on the gramophone, and red sails drift past on the azure sea. Spaghetti is being cooked; meat, fish and strawberries to follow. As it gets dark, the lights flash on across the Bay, and in the town. Rowing boats swish by, the occupants singing in glorious voices.

Next Day, 6th June
Last night after leaving the restaurant we motored up the hill to that dancing place called the Orange Grove. It has a large garden terrace which commands the most beautiful view of the Bay. The trees all have little coloured lights among the leaves, and the moon shines down through the palms. One can dance until 12.

When we arrived here it came through on the radio that Rome had fallen. Oh! how we cheered – at last ROME is ours. Maybe it won't be so long before I am home after all. All my love, Tim

11th June, 1944
Still nothing much doing, so managed to get the weekend off, and went to stay with Contessa di San Martino Franca at their villa at Sorrento, firstly to enjoy myself and secondly to see poor Raleigh Trevelyan, who has been wounded and is in hospital convalescing there.

... He has lived and fought under the most dreadful conditions, Mummy, ever since the beginning of March. Twice his entire platoon has been killed except for the odd man, and each time he has kept cheerful and managed with the help of Keats and Balkan Sobranie cigs to keep going. At last he is able to rest in this beautiful part of Italy. The only thing that he has found out of all this is the stupidity of this war, but thank God he is safe and I hope will be able to come on with me. We have always been together.

The Villa Angelina, Sorrento
The Villa of the Angels, I can never hope to describe its beauty. Set upon the very tip of the Sorrento peninsula with the magic Capri across the straits. It commands the most wonderful view in creation. Capri to the left, the Isle of Ischia in front and Vesuvio and Naples across the 'blue carpet' to the right. A garden of roses, geraniums, poppies and azaleas slopes away from the verandah over the rocks to the crystal-clear bay below, where one can swim in the lukewarm water. The Contessa and her husband are quite charming and speak perfect English. She is very beautiful in the typical Italian way – raven hair, olive skin, and magnificently dressed. They are both very kind and seem to like having young people around them.

Last night Raleigh came to dinner, which we had on the terrace. Perfect silver and glass on the shining table top. The dinner mats were made of the most lovely lace, and the candle shades of pink silk covered with lace. After dinner we watched the sun set. I remember the nights in North Africa with the golden rocks, but this one was even more fantastic – the sky shot with red and purple, the lights of Capri appearing as night came. Three black cormorants flew squawking by off to their homes in the rocks. As so often they made me think of Portmeirion and you. Oh how I wish you could be here with me, if only for a minute. But we must wait; one day we will come to Italy again together.

At about 10 p.m. the Contessa said that we must all swim, so off we went to change. After a good half hour she came back clad in a bottle-green satin bathing costume embroidered with pink flowers, and followed by the Count who led the way with a lantern down the pathway to the sea. The moon was up and a silver road appeared across the water. How can I describe the heavy smell of the flowers and the fireflies among the bushes? You must use your imagination. We all made garlands of azaleas and carnations, then threw them into the deep blue water and dived through the centre. The water seemed lukewarm after the cool night air, and as one swam, ripples of phosphorescent spray came to the surface. HOW CAN YOU BELIEVE ALL THIS? IT IS ALL SO FANTASTIC. Is the war real? Or is this? Or either? 'Variety is the spice of life.' Perhaps that is why beauty is so potent when one can only guess what is round the corner. SOME DAY I will wake up at home and find it is ALL a dream. All my love, Tim

I had been slightly wounded during the breakout from the Anzio Beachhead. Now, after a short spell in a Naples hospital, I was convalescing at Sorrento. It was true that I had always carried an edition of Keats's poems in my pack. *War and Peace* I had found not suitable for trench reading. In fact it had been hard to concentrate at all on the printed word.

I had lost many friends, including Charles Newton, who in many ways resembled Timmy, for his perpetual high spirits and his appreciation of the underlying beauty of the real Italy in the midst of all that carnage. I think I had learned rather more than that the war was stupid. I had grown up, and I realize this now when I read my diary entries compared to the Ranby and Algiers days. After the weather had changed, and there was mud no more, flowers had appeared at Anzio in all the most unlikely places. Peering above the rim of my 'foxhole' I could see the distant Alban Hills, where the Germans kept their giant railway gun which we called Anzio Annie. Beyond them, I knew were Frascati, Hadrian's Villa, Tivoli, the Sabine Hills. Some day I would visit all of those. Then there were the nightingales. The worse things were, the more they sang. Was this the 'music of the moon', or were they mocking us? To stop myself hating them I read and re-read, or at least tried to, that little book in my pack.

The unexpected wonder of their song was the equivalent of the fireflies at Sorrento, hundreds of them, twinkling and darting about at night in the lemon and orange groves. I had never seen anything like it. At first I had been sent to a large hotel in Sorrento itself used as the main officers' convalescent home, but was moved soon after to Villa Angelina, which was on a promontory a couple of miles out, with views just as Tim described. I was totally overwhelmed by the beauty of the setting. Elsewhere I have written about it as Villa Tamara. It was a modern villa, rather ugly really, in a garden that by day throbbed with cicadas. I could see Capri from my window. The villa belonging to Tim's friends was just below. We had listened to Debussy's *'L'Après-midi d'un faune'* on their gramophone. Whenever I hear it now I feel a slight shiver.

On arriving at Sorrento I had met several Italians, including Alberto Moravia and his wife Elsa, who had invited me and another officer in the 60th Rifles to stay with them in a rented house in Capri – officially designated as an American 'rest zone' (Ischia being British). I had been given special leave to go to Capri by our Red Cross commandant, an awesome lady, and I was still there when Tim, unknown to me, had arrived at Villa Angelina, where he had stayed the first night. At Capri, or rather Anacapri, I had discovered yet another Italy, a pre-war Italy, almost untouched by the war. Francis Brett Young's villa was next to where we were staying. All this I was able to tell Tim when we were reunited.

Within a week I was with Tim at the IRTD (Infantry Reinforcements Training Depot) at Rotondi. Jimmy Stevens and other old friends such as John Macalpine were there too.

. . . Always I seem to be enthusing, but how can one help it in this country?

Back again to the valley of the Madonna della Stella, looking enchanting now with the pale green of the chestnut trees.

Today I went to look at my 'Wild Children'. Before I got half way up the hill, there were shouts of 'TIMMI, TIMMI' from every direction, and down the hillside ran the little barefooted creatures throwing themselves at me in a frenzy of delight. Before I knew where I was, two *lire* pieces were brought out of every ragged pocket, and Mario was sent to buy vino. Another party was despatched to pick wild strawberries and cherries. Within ten minutes they were all back with their presents, and sitting round me on the grass talking all at once in broken English and pidgin Italian. Vito with his long unruly hair and dark black eyes, little Antonietta clutching a rag doll, and Domenico with his piglet on a long lead of twine. They told me that Angelo had lost his father, who was a prisoner in America and that Giuseppe had gone to Benevento to work for the English. So many little things that are life to these people.

This valley to most of my associates is ugly and squalid, why I cannot think. To me it has a hidden beauty that it is impossible to describe.

At first it does seem dirty and squalid. But when you go deep down you find a simplicity and faith that could never be called ugly. The people are strange and at first rather hostile, but that is only because the black hand of civilization, so-called, has never come their way before. Their happiness is a fundamental happiness that is given to every living thing, and of course they resent rude English soldiers commandeering their cornfields and filling their land with noises of rifle shots and grenades. Wouldn't we feel the same? No one hates being messed about more than the English, but I am sorry to say that the army never looks at the other person's point of view . . . All my love, Tim

I felt very privileged to meet the Wild Children. Their voices calling him from the woods were like the highest notes of flutes. The children skipped about us, pinching and chasing one another, and tweaking our uniforms. Of course we would not allow them to pay for the vino, and gave them some extra *lire* for their families.

We were passing through a strange interlude, for we knew that very soon we would be sent north. There was also so much to talk about. Tim told me that he and Dipsy would probably get married. He gave me an address that would reach her secret hideout in the mountains, in case anything 'happened'. My Anzio experience 'like a hideous demon' hovered always at the back of my mind, and I am afraid I spoke a great deal about it. I had to tell Toumi about my fears, and what I thought was my guilt. I was haunted by believing that I had made wrong decisions that had caused the deaths of people in my platoon who had almost become like brothers, relying on me. I was also worried about how I would behave when sent again into battle. A platoon commander was supposed to set an example, to be in front. Perhaps I upset him by being so frank. We could hide nothing from one another. Now that I compare my diary entries with his letters I am in a way amused to find so many phrases and descriptions expressed in exactly the same words. Did I copy them from him, or did he copy them from me? In those few days we were closer than ever before.

We were sent on Schemes in country that seemed unchanged since medieval times, and in the full glory of Italian summer. We camped among olive groves and in chestnut woods, looking down on cornfields and hearing church bells ringing from clusters of ochre-coloured roofs. So many of our companions, as Toumi had remarked, hated Rotondi and the string of villages along the road, more or less running into one another: Paolisi, Cervinara, Salamoni, Pirozza. They found the inhabitants surly, and sneered at the VV IL DUCEs still scrawled on walls. But Toumi and I sometimes went into local bars and cafés. We loved to hear the clopping of donkeys in the streets before reveillé, and the women chanting as they went to fetch firewood. The mind is its own place.

We went twice to Toumi's favourite restaurant, Giuseppone a Mare at Posillipo. On the first occasion I met his friends Renata and Vincenzina, chocolate-coloured sisters with black almond eyes and black hair, who swam with us and made us do underwater 'ballets'. They sang 'Lili Marlene' and made no secret of having had German boyfriends. The next time we brought two FANYs, friends of Dipsy but not serving with SOE (so they pretended); and Renata and Vincenzina tactfully kept their distance. Someone had scrounged a jeep, which the English girls decorated with bougainvillaea and oleander flowers. We drove to Pozzuoli, rather drunk, singing and waving, and made for the Solfatara, where the sulphur fumes helped to sober us. Later we went up to the Orange Grove, in time to see night fall over Naples. From there we had that famous view that appears in all nineteenth-century travel books on Italy: an umbrella pine in the foreground, Castel dell'Ovo, and wicked old Vesuvio on the curve of the Bay, biding his (or her) time. I found two boozy majors whom I had met at Anzio. They were enchanted by our FANYs, and as a result – it is a complicated story – Toumi and I found ourselves in possession of a fifteen-hundredweight truck, completely ours for the next days.

Madam, as we christened the fifteen-hundredweight, took Toumi and me, with Jimmy Stevens and John Macalpine, to see Caserta Palace. We had brought a picnic, including pink spumante and huge yellow peaches. We behaved rather badly, bathing in the great basin in the middle of which are statues of Diana and her nymphs watching Actaeon being torn to bits by his hounds.

On our return to Rotondi we were told that we were off to the Front in two days, the 29th. So Madam conveyed us to an enormous meal at Zi' Teresa's, below Castel dell'Ovo. Afterwards we went, as usual, to the Orange Grove, and there we found Nick Mosley. The band played 'As Time Goes By' for us.

30th June, 1944

There has been I am afraid, an 'enforced silence'. I can't tell you where I am except that I am with the Rifle Brigade again, thank goodness. Quite a few changes of scene lately.

Cassino   Without a single house standing. Just an endless pile of rubble and gaunt walls. The Monastery alas no more than a pile of black rocks – surrounded by graves. I passed through one night and stood for a short time looking at the silent and terrible sight. No sound except the nightingales, which sang as though nothing had happened. How callous and out of harmony they seemed, but for ever more Cassino will be a lesson to the world that there must never be another war.

The Liri Valley   Olive groves, ravines with rushing streams bubbling over waterfalls into rocky pools. Heaven for a quick dip when you are hot. No peasants left, their homes are shattered. Their fields covered with mines and burned-out vehicles. Sometimes you may see a family living in a 'Bosch' dug-out or in the ravines, but they shrink from us and won't speak. No wonder. We have pounded their blessed soil with artillery for three months or more.

Rome   Oh how lovely it is, the ideal city, wide open streets flanked with flowering oleander trees: pink white and scarlet in contrast to the grey stone buildings. Beautifully dressed women, huge hotels with smart aristocratic civilians in their splendid restaurants. How I wish I could have stayed for more than a few hours, but that must wait until the next 'job' is done.

One rather important thing. A lot of people in England have worried a great deal when they have got a telegram saying their son has been wounded. These telegrams are sent over for the smallest wounds, just scratches in fact. If I get wounded I will write as soon as possible. So Mummie darling, please don't worry. So many people get wounded; it is such a small thing these days – and few wounds are serious. The doctors are so good.

Au revoir – I love you so much and you are always with me – ALWAYS – promise me not to worry. Love to all, Tim

He was lucky to have seen Rome. I only got as far as the tomb of Cecilia Metella on the Appian Way. We camped at Terni amid weird rocks that looked like dragons, and then reached Orvieto, where there was a surprisingly civilized transit camp. The camp commandant was a man of taste, and did his best to make the food more interesting by giving us tagliatelle for lunch. The Blimps were of course up in arms, complaining about 'Wop muck'.

Three Rifle Brigade battalions, forming the 61st Infantry Brigade, were in the line ahead of us, somewhere near Perugia. It was here at Orvieto that we would be told which one of the battalions was to be our fate. As Toumi said, we were like gladiators at Pompeii waiting to have our biceps appraised and our teeth tapped. After a lot of fuss we managed to get permission to enter Orvieto to see the cathedral, only to find that the outside had been boarded over. When it was dark, we went for a swim in a small lake near the camp. The water was so warm that we bathed for half an hour. Toumi collected glow-worms which he put on a water-lily leaf and waved about like a torch. We realized, because of various statues dotted around, that we must be in the grounds of some large private house. We set out to explore, and soon came across a group of buildings. Dogs began to bark, and a terrified little man appeared with a shotgun. We decided to beat it, if only to keep the peace.

The next morning I found myself allocated to the 7 RBs, with John Macalpine. It was a great disappointment as Toumi went to the 10 RBs, where there was a number of old friends, including Jimmy Stevens, Charley Morpeth, Bubbles Nicholson, Ralph Stewart-Wilson (brother of the 'beautiful Prue') and Michael Trevor-Williams, and with Dick Southby as his colonel. A paragraph from this last letter, I have noticed, was scored out by the censor, but I can decipher two words, 'Raleigh Trevelyan'. Obviously he had said something unacceptable about our having to go to different battalions.

4th July, 1944

Just a scribble from my truck to tell you that all goes well in spite of the noise. Such a mixture too: swoosh, crump, wheeeeee, zing, crack. Then an eerie silence with only the birds singing, the crickets buzzing, and the frogs croaking by the lake side. I shall always remember this time with rather mixed feelings. Horror and excitement on the one hand, and on the other a peace of mind and an extraordinary feeling of being detached from it all. Never before has the 23rd Psalm applied so well. 'The Lord is my Shepherd'; 'Yea, though I pass through the valley of the shadow of death, I shall fear no evil.' These words ring through my head all the time. One can never tell what will be round the corner and can only trust in God to show the way and believe completely in His judgement.

Such lovely country, it seems sacrilege to spoil it. Luckily the Germans have been pushed so hard that they have had little time to wreck this area. June and May I should think are the best time of the year here. July is much too hot, and the dust is stifling. We are so fortunate not (swoosh) to have rain like the poor people in Normandy, who I hear are waist deep in mud. (Excuse the writing being so bad, but the truck vibrates with the rough roads.)

After the war, I hope everyone will have seen enough slaughter to make them realize that wars just aren't worth while.

Only three weeks ago my letters from Naples and the South must have seemed very 'peacetime'. It is extraordinary that you seem much nearer to me than our friends the Germans, who are just across the way. It is I suppose through God we can always feel the people we most love in times like these.

Mummie, you must *not* worry about me. I am quite happy in myself about the future, and *whatever* happens we both know that it is for the best. I haven't had any letters from you for about two weeks now as I have been travelling, but found when I got here 1000 cigarettes from you! How they got to this address, I don't know, but anyway they were a godsend, as I was rather low myself, and my men were very short. Thank you so much.

Charley Morpeth has been doing very well out here, but was very bruised having been dragged from his vehicle by civilians, hysterically happy at being freed from the Bosch. They are amazing: flowers, fruit, wine thrown at us when we take a place, weeping, kissing. Oh, how dotty it all is. *So* like a film, rather a long one though.

All my love my darling Mummie. Will write soon. Tim

We passed Chiusi and Montepulciano, the land of the Etruscans, then we camped near Lake Trasimene: too reedy for bathing. 6 July would be my twenty-first birthday. I wrote of the quiet, gentle colours of Tuscany, the cypresses, the fields wreathed in vines, and the red pantiles of farmhouses – trying to put out of my mind that soon we were going to drive on to Arezzo. The Germans were putting up strong resistance above Castiglion Fiorentino. Nevertheless there was a lot of optimism – 'We've got the whiphand over Jerry'. I confess that I was disappointed with the men in my platoon. They were nearly all older than me, or seemed like it. Those who had fought in the Desert were cynical or downright bolshie. They obviously thought I was a poor replacement for their last officer, who had been killed, and were the more suspicious because I was regarded as 'fresh', which would mean that we might have to lead an attack. Elsewhere I have written that Toumi, knowing my feelings, had 'characteristically offered to take my place', when it was known that my platoon would indeed be about to go into the attack. What I said was not quite true, or indeed possible, as we were in different battalions. I had seen him briefly, and he had said that he wished he could have taken my place. He also said we would celebrate my birthday when we reached Florence.

10th July, 1944

I do hope you got my last letter written in pencil, I entrusted it to a Rifleman to post.

I am out of the line for a day or so to rest, and am only too relieved, after five days without sleep and having to be on watch the whole time. I don't like resting for too long, as one gets relaxed and is too inclined to worry about 'the why, which, wherefore and how', if you know what I mean – one probes too deeply. This last 'duffy', as the men call it, has been rather a strain, as you will have seen by the news. Life has not been easy, with heavy opposition, and the thing that has been difficult is taking over completely 'green' men who have never been in action before. But I have been lucky with them on the whole, touch wood. I am sorry to say, on top of the other worries, Raleigh Trevelyan has been wounded again, this time I am afraid badly. Multiple fracture of the arm, and shrapnel in the head and face, also I believe some in his thigh. I can't get any news of him at all, which is most worrying. You know how very fond I am of him, and even in this callous and hard state one is inclined to be over-depressed at times. But now I have acquired a sort of steel wall, which I hope cannot be penetrated, even by the worse thing. This I am sure is the only answer, as otherwise one would be hurt at every corner. When you think things out level-headedly afterwards, you are alright, but it is the initial blow that must at all costs be repulsed. You taught me that when Daddy died.

Never for a minute did you relax your guard or show your real feelings. My outlook is based as much as possible on yours. I could not ask for a better example.

My new position commands the most wonderful view. The slit trench, which holds myself and batman, is rather a makeshift affair, under a stunted holly tree that twists and twines over our heads. Clumps of yellow broom and cypress trees stretch away down the rugged hillside to the cultivated valley below, where a little medieval town with a castle and twisting streets clings to the foothills. How peaceful it all looks, and how far away. But all today the Germans have shelled the town and reduced most of it to smouldering ruins. As I write this, shells whine overhead and crash round our position and into the town.

Now and again, through the clamour comes the sound of church bells from the monastery on the hill, where the monks and peasants pray for the liberation of their valley from war. How good they sound, a light in the darkness, an assurance that there is still something solid and worthwhile in this world of hatred and fear. More and more each day I realize the true value of religion. In everyday life it is essential, but here one realizes only too well that without it all is lost. Without it one would be like a ship without a compass in a stormy sea, not knowing which way to turn and whom to rely on for guidance.

Perhaps this is the most important time of my life. I am learning the most important things of life in a very short time. In a way that proves without doubt every lesson that I learn. I am having opportunities that for some people will never be possible, to lay a sound and solid foundation in my heart for life in the future. No matter what happens on the surface, my anchor will from now on always be there.

So don't worry about me, instead be happy and thankful that I am here and that I am finding my final goal – that is the only thing that matters. This life is such a small thing in eternity. I hope you understand this; it is badly put because words cannot describe feelings.

I have told you because I will never hold things back from you. All my love, Timmy

On the 5th 10 RB had tried to clear Monte Maggiore above Castiglion Fiorentino and had failed. So 7 RB was sent forward, and we dug our shallow trenches on the reverse slope. Just before light, Toumi, to my amazement, came crawling over with a large key. 'Many happy returns. Here's the key of the door. The champagne from Fortnum's will follow.' He was wearing camouflage netting – a hair-net he called it – over his tin hat, and I remember thinking that his face looked blotchy. That night the enemy attacked. It was a great muddle, grenades exploding, Very lights in all directions. The result was that I was hit by a shell from our own artillery in the valley below.

12th July, 1944

I wrote you yesterday, but as I have a bit of time this evening, I thought I would have another chat with you. We are still resting and I am feeling on top of the world, after sleeping for twelve hours. I have made a very comfortable little 'bower' out of ground sheets and branches from the wood where we are camped. The life in this wood is indeed pleasant after the past hard week. From my 'window' I can see the shirtless suntanned men cooking their meals and washing their clothes in the leafy coolness. The vehicles even fit in now that they are draped with camouflage nets. I keep on feeling that at any moment Pan will appear, and turn all the men into satyrs or gremlins or something. This wood is, I am sure, the enchanted wood from 'Dear Brutus'.

There is an extraordinary feeling among these men, who are resting and waiting to go back to battle; a feeling of comradeship and loyalty, and of course relief that they have at least seen the end of one more 'duffy'. They lie on the grass writing home to their families and friends, and listening to the wireless – a programme from England – English girls' voices – English music. For two, or perhaps three, whole days one can be at peace. Three days to us is a lifetime.

I am giving a small 'soirée' for my friends this evening: fried chicken, corn on the cob, and goat's milk cheese – all procured by my faithful batman Kean. He is a first class man and has a knack of knowing just what I want at the right time. Charley Morpeth, I am sorry to say, lost two fingers in the last action, so will not be here. I miss him very much. He has done wonderfully well and the men all adore him.

My letters must seem horribly self-centred I am afraid, but it is so difficult to think about things outside one's immediate surroundings – except about you and the family. Though I haven't heard from you for some while I can sense that all is well. It is nine months today since I sailed from England. So much has happened that I feel it is nine years.

I enclose a couple of photos taken sometime in March, which I thought you might like. One is of Jimmy Stevens and self on bullocks (!), going for a picnic, and the other a close-up of Jimmy and self. I thought I would send you as many photos as possible, because when Kit was away, I remember you were always wanting them. Anyway if there are too many, the aunts might like one or two. . . . I have no time to write to anyone else but you.

All my love Mummsie darling, Timmy

For me, it had been hospital again in Naples, and then back to Sorrento, and ultimately Villa Angelina once more. Charley joined me at Sorrento, also one or two other Rifle Brigade officers who had been wounded. Toumi had written to me to say that he had rescued my diary. I had been keeping a diary since school, and had always been in dread of anyone reading it. Better Toumi than anyone else, I realized, even if there were things in it that I would have preferred him not to see. From then onwards I stopped keeping a regular diary.

18 July, 1944

A short note to let you know that I am O.K.

I am sitting in a vineyard outside my truck, cooling off after a sweltering day. How lovely it is to relax and watch the dying sun. A delicious smell of frying chicken is coming from the ditch where my faithful batman is cooking the evening meal. The rest of my headquarters are laying the dinner table (an old ammunition box) and cleaning their weapons. In fact all is peaceful and quiet except for the rumble of guns ahead. This is a moment of sheer happiness – a feeling of contentment and that one's job for a few hours is done.

Today was an exciting day. As you will have seen from the news our advance has been held up for some time by very stubborn resistance round a town in the central sector [Arezzo]. Now at last we have broken it, and this morning my platoon entered the town with the first tanks. A grand reward. The main streets crowded with people shouting and cheering us. One woman climbed onto my vehicle and had to be removed by the police. Most embarrassing for me, as the whole platoon was shouting, 'Kiss 'er, Sir, 'Ave a go, Sir'. Which I did!! So all was well. The people threw flowers, gave us bottles of wine, fruit, eggs. Not surprising when one thinks about it, because for them the war is over. The Germans have taken all the nice household goods with them and most of the food. When I think that this might have happened in England, I thank God we were spared. The destruction is appalling. Even churches are ransacked.

The extraordinary thing about this war is that the feeling of comradeship and happiness between us is greater than I could have believed possible. The men are *terrific*. There is always tea made if we stop for more than ten minutes. My bed is out of the truck and made if we are certain of stopping for two hours or so. When we do work for forty-eight hours or longer without a break or sleep they are cheerful and never give in to fatigue. I am lucky with my platoon. I couldn't wish for a better lot of men. How I hate the thought of losing them.

No news of Raleigh Trevelyan, which is trying. If only I could get some sort of indication that he is alright it would be better. Maybe tonight I shall hear. Charley Morpeth I am pleased to say has only lost one finger, and was better yesterday I heard – so that is good.

How I hope the war will end soon. The destruction is so pointless. It must never, never be allowed to happen again. There are too many lovely things in the world to be seen and done to waste one's life on the battlefield in the cause of destruction. I long to create something again, so I draw quite a lot – just little sketches of places and our doings. But there is so little time to do anything really satisfactory.

Au revoir, my darling Mummie. Please look after yourself, and don't worry about me. You can see from my letter that I am in the best of form. Love to Everybody. Tell David I now have a Leica camera. All my love, Tim xxxxxx

This was his last letter to his mother. He was killed very early in the morning of 26 July near Renacci, a village on high ground north of the River Arno, near San Giovanni Valdarno. Jimmy wrote to tell me, and then more letters arrived.

It was raining on the day that Jimmy's letter came, unusual for August. It was waiting for me at Villa Angelina, on my return from Sorrento where I had actually posted a letter to Tim, written in our usual crazy style. For some while I was paralysed, very cold. Then I went up to my room, and stayed there for most of the day, facing the view of Capri through those grey, streaked, window-panes: Capri, which he had missed and would have loved. After a few days I wrote down all that I felt about Tim.

I was told that just before midnight on the 25th his company had attacked in some orchard country, and that they had run into Spandau fire. Tim and his platoon had been sent to find a way round to the right. He had lost his way among the thickets and narrow valleys and had realized that there were men in a farm building. A voice had called out 'Italiani', so Tim advanced, assuming that they were partisans. But they were German paratroopers and Tim was shot at five yards' range. There were six other casualties in the platoon, all killed.

The letters written about Tim after his death were kept by the family. Dick Southby wrote, remembering him also at York. He said: 'His death is to me the biggest personal loss among the number of officers who have inevitably fallen since this campaign began.' Vic Turner, our colonel from Ranby, wrote of the distress that the news would cause Mike King, who was in Germany, and giving the names of three others of our contemporaries who had also just been killed in Germany. There were letters from Robert Fellowes and Deedy Darley. 'He was always so full of life,' Robert wrote, 'It is quite impossible to think of him in any other way. I shall never forget him, or his real joie-de-vivre.'

This was Jimmy Stevens's letter:

Dear Mrs Lloyd,
   . . . Timmy was one of my greatest friends, both in England and when he joined us out here, and I thought perhaps you would like me to write and tell you about everything.
   Timmy came to us during one of our hardest times, but settled down very well, and I think he was very happy. His men were devoted to him, and would follow him anywhere. It was during an attack that Tim so tragically met his end. He was given a very important task of getting on to a hill, and with great courage and

determination set out to fulfil it. . . . I know it would help you to know he died instantly and felt no pain.

He was buried by the side of the road, and though unfortunately I was not present at the funeral, I went along afterwards. I managed to gather a huge bunch of wild flowers, white, yellow and mauve and put them on his grave. They really looked very lovely, and I think it is what Tim would have desired, he was so fond of wild creatures, and anything to do with the countryside.

I can't tell you how it hurts to tell you all this, and I feel very deeply for you.

There is one thing that we can be thankful for, he had a very happy life. He was so gay and imaginative and loved by all. I shall always cherish the memories of times spent with him and the fun we had. I feel he would want us to carry on as before, so we must bear it bravely. My heartfelt sympathies to you and your family.

My letter to his mother had also been kept. I said that I had had a letter from him written on 25 July, 'of course very bright and cheerful, full of the loveliness of Tuscany and how we would meet in Florence'. 'Every day, every moment,' I wrote, 'I am reminded of him. Everything I do or see that is beautiful or interesting or gay reminds me of him. For we each of us knew instinctively what would appeal to the other. He was the type of person whom everyone loved and could not help doing. His unaffected gaiety was an inspiration and practically a tradition with us all. I am sure he would want us to carry on this tradition.'

John Macalpine and Mike King wrote – Mike asking if it would be possible to have the cocktail shaker with Juke Box engraved on it. I had written to Dipsy Portman, and she too wrote to Tim's mother; so did Sue Ryder. Dipsy told Mrs Lloyd how Tim had spoken of the family, and about his embarkation leave at Pipewell. 'I hope you will not resent me saying that I loved him very much too, and it all came as the most horrible shock that I still cannot fully realize and believe it is true. . . . We always seemed fated to meet in the most fantastic way all through our travels from place to place. But religion meant a great deal to Timmy, that I feel so strongly that he is still very near to those that loved him, and because of that one must not mourn too much as he would hate it that way.' Sue Ryder in her letter talked of being on the same ship with him the previous November, and the day she spent with him among the Trulli houses. She also wrote of his 'tremendous religious faith'. In her book she quotes Dipsy's letter to her, on hearing about Tim's death. 'I believe so much,' Dipsy wrote to her, 'in not letting one's personal tragedies affect work or other people's lives; in knowing how those who have gone before would so hate one to mourn and not care for the better things in the world. But it's so hard to laugh and forget, even for five minutes – "Better by far you should forget and smile, than that you should remember and be sad" – but I think one does both.' Sue adds: 'Neither of us ever became accustomed to death.'

Postscript

I wrote to Michael Trevor-Williams asking him to rescue my diary. But Michael himself had been wounded, and it was a long time before he could reply. He told me that my diary had been sent with Tim's belongings to his mother. I wrote to Mrs Lloyd about this, but had no reply and began to despair of ever seeing it again.

Charley Morpeth lost a leg. Then, on 11 September, Jimmy stepped on a mine in an olive grove and was killed. So I had lost my three best friends in five months: Tim, Charles Newton, and now Jimmy. Robert Fellowes died, as a result of the wounds he'd had at Alamein.

In October, 1944, I went to work with the Military Mission to the Italian Army in Rome, and there I remained until I was demobilized at Christmas, 1946. In February, 1945, I had a letter from Dipsy saying that she was going to get married to an RAF officer, Guy Manning. She had been working as a radio operator. Sue Ryder has pointed out that the FANYs with SOE were only allowed to have 'platonic' relationships; so Dipsy had to have very special permission to marry. Guy was a pilot serving in the Special Duties Lysander Squadron, which dropped 'Bods', as SOE-trained agents were known, and supplies by parachute over Northern Italy for the partisans.

Dipsy told me that they were going to spend their honeymoon in Florence, but would be spending their first night in Rome.

Could we meet? I was a little surprised that she would want to do this, but of course agreed. I remember her as being very pretty, blonde, about five feet. Guy was handsome too, dressed of course in RAF uniform. I took them to the officers' night club, the Columbia in Via Gregoriana, and remember talking about ballet and how she had been a VAD before becoming a FANY. The weather was exceptionally cold, indeed icy. Early the next morning they were flying to Florence.

A little later I heard that their plane had crashed on landing, and that they had both been killed. They were buried together near Florence.

The war in Europe ended in May, 1945. I think it was only afterwards that I received a parcel marked 'Collins Publishers'. Inside was my diary, without any letter. It gave me a great shock, as I assumed that Tim's mother had sent Collins my diary hoping that they might want to publish it. Although Tim had spoken so often about his family, oddly enough I had not registered that his brother-in-law was a publisher – or if he had told me, it would have meant relatively little. I immediately set about rubbing out embarrassing bits that I had written in pencil. Some pages, however, were written in ink, and others in indelible pencil: so they survived. Those pages have helped to remind me of times I spent with Tim. Now I can destroy them.